TRAPPED

TRAPPED

*Life under Security Capitalism
and How to Escape It*

MARK MAGUIRE

AND SETHA LOW

stanford briefs
An Imprint of Stanford University Press
Stanford, California

Stanford University Press
Stanford, California

Printed in the United States of America
on acid-free, archival-quality paper

Cataloging-in-Publication Data available upon request.
Library of Congress Control Number: 2023053784
ISBN: 9781503632967 (cloth), 9781503639201 (ebook)

Cover design: Daniel Benneworth-Gray

Cover photograph: Unsplash

Typeset by Classic Typography in 11/15 Adobe Garamond

CONTENTS

PROLOGUE

Clara and Hugo woke early on the morning of Saturday, September 21, 2013. They were to host friends for dinner that evening, and a shopping trip to the busy Westgate Mall was required. The British-Kenyan couple lives in the house Clara inherited from her father in Nairobi's up-market Westlands neighborhood. The house is a colonial-era mansion designed to be approached via extensive grounds. Over the years, however, the family's holding has shrank back, yielding ground to advancing suburbs. Their wooden veranda now looks out on a modest garden, ringed by high walls and finished with barbwire. In Westlands, well-to-do residents live interior lives. They travel to and from gated homes, offices, and shopping malls in SUVs. They live in fear of intruders, carjackers, and terrorists. More precisely, they experience a sense of dread—they know their world will shatter one day.

However, that Saturday morning Clara and Hugo's minds were on the evening ahead: dinner, then bottomless glasses of wine on the colonial veranda. They aimed to spend no more than an hour shopping in Westgate.

Westgate Mall is a temple to security capitalism: it expresses in concrete and glass the force exerted by securitization, massive inequality, and the neoliberal privatization of public space. Although it occupies five aboveground floors, the mall squats on the side of Mwanzi Road, its windows squinting out from behind international brand logos. Such spaces are designed with specific customers in mind, especially those who arrive and depart by car to avoid the chaos of street life. Around noon that Saturday, Clara and Hugo's Range Rover halted on the entrance ramp, and a uniformed security guard "inspected" their vehicle by immediately waving them on. Westgate was especially busy that day. The noise from dozens of children attending a rooftop cookery competition filled the building. Clara parked in a space on the uppermost floor. At the same time, an al-Shabaab death squad entered Westgate, pausing to murder shoppers, including children, at the main entrance.

Clara heard a loud noise, but she could not figure out what was happening. The full horror of the situation dawned on Hugo:

> *People, to begin with, ran into the corner and didn't know what was going on. . . . And then they shut up very quickly when one guy started executing people, just, literally, straight in the back of the head. . . . Interestingly*

enough, it goes in waves: realization of what's going on; rushing in a panic but not necessarily a really big panic, because you haven't put two and two together about how brutal they are going to be. Then they tell you what's going to happen. Then they execute a few people, and it's, like, "Oh heck." So, there's a lot of screaming and crying, and then they execute some more, and it's, like, "Oh God!"[1]

Hugo hid under the Range Rover, while Clara hid under a smaller car in the adjacent parking space. She knew that there was little point in calling Nairobi's notoriously corrupt and ineffective police, and she suspected that the low-paid security guards were either dead or had fled. So, she sent text messages to family members while silently praying for a miracle.

A terrorist spotted Hugo and shot him where he hid. Clara stifled a scream so as not to betray her position. Though wounded and traumatized, they were among the lucky ones who survived. They lived because, at some point, a mature "European" man appeared. Holding a handgun by his side, he calmly searched for survivors. As if abiding by the terms of some secret agreement, the al-Shabaab terrorists yielded the car park to him. Like the terrorists, Clara read the scene instantly. In Nairobi, multinational corporations and very wealthy individuals employ ex-Special Forces mercenaries to provide rescue services. Clara was correct. The fearsome modern-day Praetorian retrieved his client and scooped up Clara, Hugo, and a dozen other "Europeans," before exiting via an emergency stairwell. As Clara half-walked, half-carried

Hugo down the stairs, she heard gunfire, and the screams resume on the floor above her.

How did we end up here? We are now discussing the price of security when here it denotes living behind walls or even paying for the privilege of rescue by a ferocious mercenary. Many people spend money on gates and guards these days; growing numbers are investing in surveillance technologies; others let the state and the police deliver violence on their behalf as a bureaucratic service. Of course, others pay a far higher price: security incarcerates, tortures, and kills many people to grant liberty to a few. This book adds to a growing body of thought about the problem of security in the contemporary moment.

Right now, there is a crisis in policing in many societies. Moreover, people are calling for an end to crisis-prone military adventures abroad and mass surveillance at home. The often nefarious role of major arms companies and shadowy security bureaucracies in each of these domains must be exposed and challenged. Social scientists have been quick to show how securitization is experienced in everyday life, especially by vulnerable communities. This effort to ground discussion is doubtless necessary. However, the effect of this positioning, together with the traditional social-scientific focus on institutions, has been to treat each area—policing, surveillance, international security, and counterterrorism—as distinct.[2] But security traverses these seemingly separate domains, connecting them, and transforming them at a deep level.

Moreover, security is not just a force exercised from above by a Big Brother whose strings are pulled by dark-money puppet masters. Rather, security works through society, vertically and horizontally. Many people feel that security is a basic need, the force that holds chaos at bay; others welcome the feeling it elicits.[3] Therefore, we must speak to the people willing to pay the blood tribute demanded, the people who buy security capitalism's latest gadgets, elect law-and-order politicians, and keep the machinery going. We argue that failure to understand security in all its supply and demand forms will lead to narrow "solutionism" and the inevitable failure of efforts to challenge the overall system. Therefore, the opening chapters of this book address those who seek out the interior world of security capitalism. Later, we turn to policing, counterterrorism, and homeland security, security capitalism's construction sites. This book is about the full cost of locking oneself inside a fortified space, turning on surveillance cameras, and hoping for a peaceful life.

But how does one initiate a conversation with people like Hugo and Clara about how they ended up trapped in a cage of their own making? A decade after the Westgate attack, Hugo's wounds still pain him. In conversation, he seems anxious and exhausted. Clara's response to the horror in Westgate is even more striking. She went out of her way to befriend the ferocious mercenary who saved her life that day. For his part, he believes they share a bond now, and he feels able to talk to her about experiences that only someone who has "been there" would understand. Clara sleeps better at night knowing that she can summon professional violence. This is a tactic rather than a strategy, a response rather than a way out. In truth, Clara and Hugo do not want to live as they do. In conversation, they fluently deconstruct life on their socially constructed veranda. Yet they are trapped there by the same conditions that produced it—colonialism, ingrained racism, inequality, institutional failure, and, above all else, a feeling that change is impossible. Yet, if offered the opportunity, they would not move house.

What to do? We do not hold a secret key that will unlock these complex structures and set people free. However, anthropological insights may help bring down the walls that divide us. This book scrutinizes people's cultural investments in institutions and the values that guide their investment choices. We go beyond narrow solutionism in search of new thinking about seemingly intractable problems.

Each chapter of this book describes things as they are in public safety, policing, counterterrorism, and homeland security, to stimulate a conversation about how things ought to be. In our experience, representing decades of ethnographic research in multiple regions, people like Clara and Hugo are ready to talk. They were the lucky ones, after all, and they know it. Hundreds of people died during the horrifying attack on Westgate. Very few could afford bodyguards or rescue by elite mercenaries. Most were members of the army of poor cleaners, child-minders, assistants, and attendants who maintain the interior world of security capitalism. Some were so poor—members of an undocumented underclass—that no one bothered to catalog their remains.

Today, many people want to talk about change, inside and outside the walls, up in the towers occupied by the elite, and down on the "chaotic" streets. Conversations are starting about societal investment in counterterrorism, surveillance, and brutal policing institutions. We are sure that meaningful change will only come when we recognize that all these areas face a common challenge—to escape the security trap.

TRAPPED

In early 2012, a teenage boy traveled with his father to Sanford, Florida, to spend time with his prospective stepmother. They intended to stay as her guests in Retreat at Twin Lakes, a small, gated community. During the evening, the boy walked to a nearby 7-Eleven convenience store, where he bought a bag of Skittles and a can of fruit juice. It was a dark, rainy evening, so he pulled up his hood, dialed his girlfriend on his mobile phone, and started for home. A short time later, a neighborhood watch volunteer passed by in an SUV and phoned the police to report a "suspicious guy." Against the dispatcher's advice, the neighborhood watchman, George Zimmerman abandoned his vehicle and pursued the boy on foot. Minutes later, following a brief altercation, seventeen-year-old Treyvon Martin lay dead from a single gunshot wound.

Initially, the tragic killing attracted little public attention. Indeed, the media depicted the whole incident as a regrettable accident, like a car crash, but with the child being mowed down by security. Retreat at Twin Lakes was supposed to be a haven of middle-class prosperity and safety, but foreclosures, short-term letting, and burglaries increased following the 2008 recession. Residents became fearful, and some openly spoke of their intention to shoot home invaders. After all, people purchased houses in this enclave to avoid what they perceived as an increasingly chaotic and crime-ridden world. However, the security measures came in the form of anti-social design features that separated residents from the outside and each other. Retreat at Twin Lakes has plenty of fences, surveillance cameras, and alarms but few public spaces and even fewer sidewalks. The designers turned walking into a suspicious activity, and the trigger-happy neighborhood watch turned racialized suspicions into potential fatalities.

Consistent with Florida's so-called stand-your-ground law, a trial jury acquitted George Zimmerman. Activists first uttered the phrase Black Lives Matter to express collective rage at the acquittal of a man who racially profiled and confronted a child. Their rage gave birth to an international movement. Around the world, from New York to Nairobi and from London to Los Angeles, there are calls to end violent, racialized policing and replace it with socially just public safety.[1] To answer this call, scholars and activists are hunting for alternatives to modern policing. Surely things were done differently in the past, or perhaps alternative models exist in other countries? Reformers are searching for training programs and interventions to reduce police violence, but many of these "solutions" are ineffective, or they further inflate already bloated police budgets.[2] Abolitionists are searching for new models of community safety, but they are accused of naïvety by a political class wedded to the status quo and comfortable with failure. It is abundantly clear that the problem of security is central to all of this, but it has yet to receive the attention it deserves. Security precedes the development of modern policing; security providers operate at the shadowy institutional borders of policing today, and if policing as we know it ends, security actors are ready to offer their services.

It is illustrative to recall that in the wake of the murder of George Floyd in 2020, Minneapolis pledged to defund its police force and reconstitute it as a public safety service. Despite the fanfare surrounding the pledge, only a few symbolic actions followed before the City Council voted down the proposal to defund the police in 2021. Nonetheless, private security operators immediately flooded into the perceived gap. Today, there are thirteen private security guards for every police officer in downtown Minneapolis. In the wealthiest suburbs, residents may avail of a "buyback" program to hire off-duty police to patrol their neighborhoods.

Before modern policing, we had Pinkerton detectives for the wealthy and vigilante patrols for the oppressed and enslaved. People in the Global South still live with a mixed security economy. In Nairobi, for example, small business owners hire off-duty police to protect them from their on-duty colleagues. As we learned in the Prologue, the wealthy enlist the services of expatriate mercenaries. In short, once interrogated, the modern institution of policing reveals itself as the child of a large family of security providers, kindred with whom it remains in suspiciously close contact. Of course, many of these security providers are just low-level players in the domain of security capitalism. However, this domain stretches from those who sell house alarms to retirees to those who sell autonomous weapon platforms to states. To understand the central problem of security in today's world, we must attend to security capitalism.

Of course, security is not simply supplied to an unknowing and unthinking public by shady businesses. We must understand the supply of security solutions, and the ascendency of "solutionism" in public discourse, but we also need to understand the demand for security. People are willing to go to great lengths to feel safe; they are willing to pay for that feeling, even if they must pay with the blood of others. "The wealthy drool for security," Ayn Rand once declared, but the middle classes are also keen investors in security capitalism. Yet, they feel trapped by security, unsafe yet unwilling to do things differently. This is where we see hope for change. As Angela Davis put it, the challenge is to persuade those people that "safety, safeguarded by violence, is not really safety."[3]

TRAPPED

This book starts from the position that security is not just about state police and private security guards, uniformed soldiers, and shadowy contractors. Rather, it is the primary activity of whole branches of government and entire sectors of the economy. Organizations that deliver policing, governance, surveillance, and international stability are fundamentally security actors. Of course, we are not the first to note this. In *Leviathan,* Thomas Hobbes argues that nature, chaotic and brutish, will never provide security, and a small community will always struggle to protect its members. Security, he explains, is the primary duty of the State, so long as you give obedience in return.[4] Jean-Jacques Rousseau expands on this basic formulation by imagining security as liberty's shield. "It is . . . a fundamental maxim of political law," he tells us, "People gave themselves chiefs to defend their liberty and not be enslaved by them. If we have a prince, said Pliny to Trajan, it is in order that he may keep us from having a master."[5] Karl Marx is similarly clear on the primacy of security. Upon reading the lofty *Declaration of the Rights of Man*, he notes, "Security is the supreme social concept of civil society. . . . The whole society exists only in order to guarantee for each of its members the preservation of his person, his rights and his property."[6] The modern police, he tells us, is just one institutional form that follows society's functional need to protect rights-bearing property owners.[7] For the sake of brevity, in this book, we refer to this as *security capitalism.*

Westgate Mall in Nairobi and Retreat at Twin Lakes in Florida are both spaces of security capitalism—privatized, fortified, unequal—even though they are thousands of miles apart. Such places are experienced as similar because their walls and fences are designed to do the same job, to produce a safe interior by keeping the chaotic outside world at bay. However, the separation between inside and outside is illusory. Things must be bought and sold, and people must come and go, so security denotes not just the effort to contain and control but, precisely, to track human activity—everything is a potential target of security. Security capitalism is thus broader and more encompassing than "surveillance capitalism," Shoshana Zuboff's catchy label for Silicon Valley's business model.[8] Though it is broader and more encompassing, security capitalism is also a more accurate term, as it explodes the myth that the digital industrial economy is the product of brilliant minds working in Palo Alto garages. Silicon Valley is the child of the US military-industrial complex, and recent high-profile leaks in companies like Facebook and Twitter show that it never flew the nest.[9] Just as security precedes the development of modern policing, we also find that security capitalism precedes and structures surveillance capitalism.

Our aim in *Trapped* is to develop ethnographic portraits of life under security capitalism, the sites into which it has spread, where alternative possibilities still flourish, and thus the spaces where we can begin to contemplate escape. Much of our work as anthropologists during the past two decades has been about the intractable problem of security in various societies. Mark's research has explored biometric security in the Middle East, predictive policing in the UK, and counterterrorism in Europe and Africa. Setha studies the rise of gated communities in multiple countries, the politics of public space, and the violent consequences of inequality and segregation. Together we have written about the spaces of security that now striate public life, spaces that erect walls between the few and the many.[10]

The ethnographic portraits of security capitalism we present here will show its supply and demand sides. We describe the growing security-industrial complex, the heartland of security capitalism, and the people who work there. Many are willing workers who are devoted to their role, while others are sickened by duplicity and corruption. We describe how security capitalism trickles down into society's infrastructure, poisoning how the public sees travel, public space, and, ultimately, one another. Security capitalism has also transformed modern policing, we argue, diminishing its few redeeming qualities and making genuine reform harder to achieve. Uniquely, this book emphasizes the demand for security capitalism. Corporate interests and political machinations certainly shape the security landscape. However, ordinary, middle-class people populate the land. They seek safety in gated suburbs and urban enclaves, and, in so doing, they create investment opportunities for security capitalism. Various "solutions" are presented to reduce anxiety and uncertainty and prevent chaos. The desire is to produce a safe "interior life," to borrow from philosopher Peter Sloterdijk.[11] Ethnographically, we open these interiors and find people trapped in prisons of their own making.[12] We must empathize with people like Clara and Hugo, the couple introduced in the Prologue, and the great multitude of others like them, while also holding them to account.

LIFE UNDER SECURITY CAPITALISM

This book unfolds over several short chapters. Each chapter provides an ethnographic portrait of security capitalism. We hope that our use of ethnographic essays will permit readers to understand the contemporary security landscape as a knotted and thorny place populated by diverse people. Nevertheless, when one stands back, the landscape does have several salient features that demand attention. In *Trapped*, we often speak of interior life, the anxieties that interiority produces, the solutions presented by security capitalism, and the security-industrial complex. We mention these concepts in the ethnographic essays where it is apt to do so. However, we also include brief notes on these concepts separate from the main chapters. The concept notes are guides to aid interpretation and, we hope, spur action.

Chapter 1, "Open the Gates, or You'll Never Escape," plunges us straight into the fears of crime, terrorism, and even noise and chaos, that ostensibly motivate people to move to gated suburban communities in New York and San Antonio, Texas. On close inspection, however, it becomes evident that fear is not the only explanation for this decision. Wealthy and middle-class people who wish to reside in gated communities are screened for financial well-being and social acceptability by homeowners' associations and common interest developments. When they purchase a home, they buy into enclosure, surveillance, financial restrictions, and aesthetic choices. The price of voluntary imprisonment is high, but the residents pay to live with other "nice" people. They say they feel better having moved to a secure residential area and rarely want out, but they experience tremendous anxiety and doubt. They doubt the efficacy of security measures, especially because separation from the outside is more theoretical and symbolic than actual: caregivers, construction workers, and other service providers enter the gated community daily. Interior life in a gated community involves "fear talk"—rumors about criminals working for construction crews, for example. In the United States, all of this is structured by racialization, sometimes overtly, at other times coded as "nice people" versus "outsiders." With the gated community, security makes physical, and thus naturalizes, racialization.

However, the decision to retreat to a homogenous racial and class redoubt does not suggest defiant middle-class strength. Whereas once the American dream was of home ownership, picket fence and all, and integration into a functioning society, today neoliberalism and globalization expose the cruel optimism of yesterday's dreams. The gated community offers life in diminished form. Security from the chaotic outside is pretended, performed, but never absolute. Residents fret about workers from the outside because the walls and gates cannot sever relations with society. On the contrary, gated communities play an outsized role in society, diverting resources, and contributing to racialized segregation and societal fracturing. The only way out of the security trap is to bring communities back into societies, which may mean some people have to face their fears and live differently.

Chapter 2, "Take Back the City: Security as a Way of Life in New York City," brings us to Hudson Yards, New York City's sparkling new commercial and residential enclave. Opened just before the COVID-19 pandemic hit, the enclave is part of the largest private real-estate development in US history. The enclave is staggeringly expensive, trendy, Instagram-able, and clearly disconnected from the rest of the city—Hudson Yards is in but not of New York. The city authorities provided tax cuts and rapid permissions, while developers promised revitalization by attracting the "right kind of people." Today, there are no bustling crowds in Hudson Yards, no chaotic city noises. The right kind of people expect to walk risk-free from their purpose-built metro station to shops or restaurants under the watchful eye of private guards and surveillance cameras. It is like a huge outdoor airport terminal.

Hudson Yards exists because of the financialization of the city. Private investors are required for major development projects. Rather than giving back to the city, however indirectly, urban life is cut up and sold to a cosmopolitan elite, who demand securitization, and this further undermines the city. The more securitization and spatial separation are permitted, the more the cycle continues. Plainly we must challenge this, but we cannot do so by appealing nostalgically for the return of earlier forms of capitalism. Today's securitization is fueled by a history of national insecurity, fear, and racialized fearmongering, and the financial insecurity that drives the city to private developers goes back to the near bankruptcy of the 1970s. All the cameras and guards, then, point to a population stuck in deep ontological insecurity. But what was the alternative to Hudson Yards? If cities commit to equitable development for the good of the public, alternatives abound. We can develop accessible public spaces, funded by a diverse array of commercial and residential units. Things can be better, but nothing will change if we continue to fund securitization.

Chapter 3, "Reimagine Policing," returns to the core problem introduced in our opening discussion of the killing of Treyvon Martin. Activists, especially Black scholars, have successfully highlighted the problem of racist police violence. Their efforts to challenge the legitimacy of modern policing are ongoing, though meaningful change remains elusive, as if there are no reasonable alternatives. Before attempting to transform policing, we must grapple with the intractable problem of societal security. Time and again, we have seen the desire for public security used as a barrier to meaningful change. But what does it mean to approach policing as a security problem. Where do we begin?

In this chapter, we trace the ethnographic story of Liam, a traditional Irish police officer—Ireland is where modern policing first developed—who recently turned his hand to consulting. His varied career involved community policing during an anti-terror war. Later, he spearheaded a mini–War on Drugs in a poor neighborhood. Later still, following a period in management, he began a career as an international security consultant. The ethnographic description of each period shows the degree to which policing is not a singular activity by an ideal-type modern institution but, rather, a fractured and violence-prone system that requires constant monitoring and reference to guiding principles. Despite all the metrics and audits that promise transparency and control, there is insufficient monitoring of policing today. Instead, modern policing is merging with private security interests, "solutionism" is ascendant, and guiding principles are forgotten. We hope that our ethnographic portrait of Liam's varied career will alert us to the core problem of principles in modern policing. Scholars have long argued that inequality breeds securitization, but here we show that security is, by its very nature, antagonistic to equality. We can strive for public safety, equality, and justice, or we can retreat in groups behind walls protected by police, but we cannot do both.

Chapter 4, "Counter Counterterrorism," is an ethnographic portrait of the forces driving and resisting security in the modern airport. Today's privatized and securitized urban enclaves resemble airports: only verified persons may enter these stratified interior worlds where calm commercialism replaces the chaos of everyday sociality. The airport has long been a laboratory for testing and producing new security systems—what happens in LAX today happens in LA tomorrow. Thus, it is essential to identify and examine the continuities and contradictions produced by security capitalism in airport-laboratory conditions.

This chapter follows the story of Steve, an upper-mid-ranking police officer in a major international airport. As he sees it, his job is to keep airplanes and their passengers moving safely. He characterizes himself as a community police officer. However, the security experts orbiting Steve's world regard him as a mere "practitioner," the "end user" of their conceptual and technical solutions. For these experts, the mundane work of keeping the peace is uninteresting. Instead, applied academics, technologists, and representatives of significant corporations drive the introduction of new products, often regardless of efficacy. As Steve's ethnographic story unfolds, however, we see not just an alliance between profit-seeking security-capitalist interests but also an entire pseudo-scientific edifice—theories about radicalization, the efficacy of mass surveillance, and mysterious detection techniques.

Desirous of less risk and more security, the public (strangely) accepts pseudo-scientific security theories.[13] To effectively counter counterterrorism, we must challenge the counterterrorism edifice at home, in our universities, and explore alternative approaches, which may be already available locally. If we can counter counterterrorism in high-stakes environments like airports, then it can be challenged anywhere.

Chapter 5, "Reclaim Homeland Security," tracks the rise of the European homeland or internal security sector by following the career of Sarah, a former Big Tech executive who reinvented herself as a security expert during the early 2000s. European countries have long been key players in international arms manufacturing. However, in the wake of 9/11, it became apparent to governments and industry that the European Union could play a more prominent role. Sarah opened a consultancy that forged alliances across national and sectoral lines, capturing significant resources as she did so. The growth of European homeland security followed a definite plan crafted and implemented by the security-industrial complex. The plan required large-scale societal cooperation from police, airport managers, policymakers, and the public. Consultants like Sarah worked feverishly to create the necessary connections and cooperation. Big Brother relies on many "ordinary" educated and middle-class helpers who buy into security capitalism. Sarah averted her gaze as European and North American colleagues sold their surveillance wares alongside old-fashioned weapons of war. However, when she watched the EU use the public purse to pay for technology to spy on citizens, she could no longer ignore the damage. She became an activist. As we follow her career in and out of the security-industrial complex, we show that security capitalism ultimately relies on public acceptance, access to public universities, and the public purse.

The Conclusion, "Defund Security," sets out our vision for change. Here we argue that there are surprisingly straightforward ways to challenge urban fortification, violent policing, and counterterrorism. We know that urban fortification compounds social divisions and inequality and damages social cohesion and democracy. The people who seek out gated communities and exclusive city enclaves know that they are separating themselves from mainstream society. However, gates do not guarantee security, and abandoning a society that one is still deeply invested in has clear consequences. Many people now feel trapped in a prison of their own making, and not just in their homes.

1 OPEN THE GATES, OR YOU'LL NEVER ESCAPE

The suburbs in the United States are notorious for restrictive zoning laws, exclusionary covenants and homeowners' associations, mortgage redlining, and other real estate discriminatory practices rooted in the Jim Crow past. Indeed, US suburbs continue to refuse to accommodate affordable housing and mixed-use planning in an attempt shut out "others," particularly Black but increasingly Latino and other minority buyers.[1] Local restrictions are part of a long history of housing segregation rationalized by governments and residents to keep their communities "safe" and "secure."

Gated communities emerged in the late 1960s and 1970s and grew in number during the 1980s and 1990s to ensure greater sociospatial control as these planning and financial laws were challenged and the economics of infrastructure development required greater private investment. We compare two gated communities—one in the suburbs of Long Island in New York State and the second in the suburban ring around San Antonio, Texas—to illuminate how fear talk and a desire for security reproduces a racist past reworked by contemporary neoliberalism and "racial neutral" politics. The resulting security-scape, however, is dangerous for all.

SUBURBAN LONG ISLAND, NEW YORK

It is hard to find the house, since they all look so similar—part of the appeal of an architecturally curated environment—but we[2] finally locate the rambling one-story home. Elizabeth Lee,[3] a woman in her late forties, short, slim, wearing a plaid shirt and hiking shorts, invites us in and begins by talking about her happiness at having moved in two months ago:

Elizabeth: *It's a happiness I can't put into words. It's being able to come home, late at night, by myself and know that I can go into a garage, and I don't have to look around and say, "Who's following me home?"*

Elena: *So, it sounds like you had your reasons.*

Elizabeth: *Practically. When Bloomingdales moved out and Kmart came in, the area changed . . . The stores kept going out [of business] and we got these fast-food stores in. It just brought in a different group of people . . . And, uh . . . it wasn't the safe place that it was.*

Elena: *Is it different [in the gated community]?*

Elizabeth: *Yes, it really is. It's coming home to my house, and I hope it's safe. You never know. There are fences that people can go over . . . and whatever . . . and I hope it is.*

Elena: *How did you decide it was safe?*

Elizabeth: *Safer than where I came from. I think it's safer having a gated community. It's safer being able to get into your garage . . . they're not going to steal my car in my garage.*

Elena: *Right.*

Elizabeth: *Every time we heard an alarm go off, [in the old neighborhood] we were looking out the window . . . My son-in-law lived next door with my daughter. Their car was stolen twice. I mean, it was a constant thing. And there was this bar on the corner with motorcycles and broken beer bottles and noise through all hours of the morning [so we had to leave].*

Gerry Bolster, who lives up the street, is also concerned about crime in her previous neighborhood, but a childhood experience initiated her fears. We find her, a twenty-nine-year-old woman wearing a white tee and a short jean skirt, watering the flowers in front of her two-story home. Gerry, her husband, and young daughter are considered pioneers at Manor House[4] having bought a Newport model even before the floor plans were ready. Safety is important to her because as a little girl her family's house was broken into, and she remembers the experience vividly:

Gerry: *I was about ten, and I remember coming home with my mother and my little brother who was a year old in the car. The door was open, and my mother went in and . . . she saw him jumping out of the back window.*

*And then I have a lot of friends who live in a neighbor-
hood in Queens, and there's been more than forty-eight
robberies there in the last year and a half. And I said to
myself, those are homes with security and dogs, and this
and that.*

Setha: *Were they in gated communities?*

Gerry: *No, they're not gated. They had the alarms, and they
were getting robbed 'cause they were cutting the alarms,
the phone wires outside. So, I'm saying to myself . . . all
this is in my mind . . . and I'm saying . . . I can get
robbed. That's why I moved.*

Stories of homes being supposedly burglarized because
they were not in gated communities—even houses with
security alarms—and feeling safer with walls and gates is
a recurrent theme. Nancy Offenbach and her husband,
George, who live in a smaller townhouse development on
Long Island, though, are skeptical about the gates. They
are both in their sixties and live at the end of a row of
identical homes with Tudor wood trim. Nancy wonders
if there is an increasing sense of insecurity "all over the
place" not just in their gated development. She explains:

Nancy: *I think people are beginning to realize they are not
really safe anywhere in middle America. We have had so
much violence occurring, terrorist things, the school shootings, you know. That could be part of it, I don't know.*

George's concern, however, is about whether the gate
even makes a difference:

George: *I don't know how much security the gate is worth (laughing) . . . Some of the guards just let you fly right in. The other ones have to strip search you. So, you know what I mean . . . it really depends.*

While the Offenbachs have their doubts about the safety provided by guards and gates, the Lees and the Bolsters are convinced that their new community will protect them from being robbed or living in a "dangerous" or noisy neighborhood. The belief that gating is necessary for security is prevalent, though some residents are doubtful that gating can address what they see as a growing sense of worry and fear.

SUBURBAN SAN ANTONIO, TEXAS

San Antonio gated residents have some of the same anxieties based on their perceptions of the deterioration of the downtown area, but also voice other concerns.

Erin Masters and her husband, Ken, moved in a couple of years ago with their two children, ages six and eight. Erin is a thirty-year-old stay-at-home mom who enjoys golf and charitable activities at their church, while Ken manages a software company. They moved because of increasing crime in the city and the desire to have a nicer house, but initially, the houses in their subdivision were too expensive. They were delighted when they were able to purchase their dream house from the Resolution Trust Corporation (RTC) that sold bankrupt properties at below market price to recoup the outstanding debt.

Erin begins our conversation by describing why the gated community is safer than where she lived previously. She explains that a security guard patrols the footpaths and housing areas every hour. To enter, they drive through controlled access gates with security cameras, and a burglar alarm protects their house. She says they feel better now that they have moved.

Setha: *So, what do you fear the most?*

Erin: *[My children] getting hit by a car out here. Playing in the road. That's about it. . . . You know, I think . . . that's one of my biggest fears, to get hit by a car right in the road. Cause they're not in tune to watching and being as cautious. . . . They [other residents] just go out and come off the driveway and they never even stop to look. Since we live on a cul-de-sac you falsely have the security that no one is going to hit you. [. . .] Probably my biggest fear out here was the fear that there is all this construction going on . . . because construction workers . . . uh . . . go out, you know, [and] draw a lot of illegal aliens to work here, just you know, I guess. . . . not to stereotype it, but you see lots of burglaries going on. Like the house next door being constructed, and then you have a burglary at your house. And they can take something and watch when you come and go in. . . . During construction I would be very, very cautious. . . . Every time I went out [I worried that] a burglar would go in.*

Setha: *OK, workers concern you?*

Erin: *It's like they can slip in and slip out . . . where there's like no record of these guys at all . . . they're here today and gone tomorrow.*

Erin says that there have been two burglaries in her subdivision, and she thinks they were inside jobs. She attributes the loss of $2,000 next door to friends of the family's teenagers who visited when they had a big party. She follows the police blotter by looking up her zip code and then calls the security guards and asks, "What happened?" to keep up to date with crime in her area.

I later bump into Dona Davies, who lives down the street with her husband and three boys, ages fifteen, seven, and five. She immediately invites me in to see how she has decorated their Scottsdale-style house. Dona is a thirty-five-year-old mother who helps her husband part-time when he travels for his insurance business. Her everyday life revolves around the children—taking them to soccer practices, going to the playground, and supervising bicycling in the neighborhood. The youngest boy has been a fearful child since a murder/suicide on the next street over. In fact, they designed their home with one wall with no window for his bedroom because he is frightened by windows. Living in a gated community has made a big difference for the children. She explains that it might be a false sense of security, but still, they feel safer:

Dona: *[It's made] a world of difference. And it is the sense of security that they don't think people are roaming the neighborhood and the streets and that there's people out there that can hurt him. [. . .] They definitely have a sense of security living out here. That's what's been most important to my husband, to get the children out here where they can feel safe, and we can feel safe they could go out in the streets and not worry that someone is going to grab them. And they feel that way out here. But I have talked to my neighbors and wonder that maybe we are too lenient with them out here thinking because they're so secure, and we feel so secure and maybe that's wrong too.*

Setha: *In what sense?*

Dona: *That we may . . . you know, we've got workers out here, and we still think "oh, they're so safe out here" but you know, children get grabbed anywhere. Not only in nongated communities. It can happen anywhere. And we still have to watch them out here. And we just get a little bit lax out here, a little bit [more] than . . . than normal. And the other neighborhood that we lived [in], I never let him out of my sight for a minute. Of course, they were a little bit younger too, but I just, would never, you know, think of letting them go to the next street over. . . . It would have scared me to death, 'cause you didn't know. . . . There was so much traffic coming in and out, you never knew who was cruising the street and how fast they can grab a child. And I don't feel that way in our area at all, ever. Even though . . . that . . . that security lets them in, and they're going in and out, I don't feel that way . . . here.*

The Davis's and the Masters's focus on their children and the fear that they could be grabbed or hit by an automobile was not unique in San Antonio ever since a young girl was kidnapped and never found. Over the next five years, this fearfulness continued to surface, especially when interviewing mothers with young children. A fear of construction workers, as emphasized by Erin but also alluded to by Dona, also surfaced repeatedly. After residents mentioned this fear, they would often admit that with the workers going in and out of the community that maybe it was not very secure after all. The ambivalence of wanting to feel that the walls and gates are protective yet knowing that their expectations were unrealistic or, more to the point, that the people they were afraid of were inside the community all day long, surfaced in interview after interview.

Jeffrey and Jenna are an older couple with a large family and many grandchildren. They were cautious in choosing their home when they first moved to San Antonio and looked at everything, though they would only consider a gated community:

Jenna: *I must live in a gated community, and it must be an upscale community, and I'm not a racist and not a bigot. I guess my only bigotry is ignorance. . . . We looked at everything that was gated and there were some lovely places that were not gated that I really liked, but I couldn't allow myself to live there.*

Jeffrey adds that they are careful to keep the house locked because "it's a fool that doesn't."

Setha: *Do you have an alarm system as well?*

Jeffrey: *Absolutely.*

Setha: *Do you use it during the day as well as the evening?*

Jeffrey: *No. Here's the only thing that's on in the daytime (referring to a chime I keep hearing).*

Setha: *Oh, that little ring? Does it let you know when something is opening? (I did not know it was a signal that a door is being opened until Jeffrey confirmed my hunch.) When you go to bed, do you turn it on?*

Jenna: *When we go to bed the [entire] alarm system goes on.*

Setha: *And when you go away?*

Jenna: *Um, there would be no point in having an alarm system if you didn't use it. I put the alarm system on, for example, if I go to the hairdresser or go shopping down the street. We do put the alarm system on when we go to bed at night. It makes me feel extremely safe. We have lights that turn on and off in three or four rooms whether we are here or not. And the only way you would know that we were not here is if you walk in the morning and the newspaper wasn't picked up or if that trash can wasn't out on trash day.*

Setha: *Would people notice?*

Jenna: *No, the only people who could possibly be casing us are the laboring people or the maids. We have to be very aware of who we let in our house and how much information they have about our house. I have had the same maid since I have been here. I trust her, but I put away my jewelry on the days that she's here. I put my jewelry in the safe. I see no point in challenging her. This is not fair to her. She is poor, and never has any hope of anything except social security. And I think I am safe with her, but I wouldn't give her the keys to my house. Not that kind of safe.*

Jenna and Jeffrey represent an extreme version of distrust of others. They also illustrate some of the many layers of protection considered usual, such as having an alarm and safe and using both to hide valuables when leaving the premises or when even a well-known worker enters the house. The level of distrust of those living outside the walls and gates was palpable. When a mother described how her daughter fears workers when they venture outside the community, the depth of this fear of others and its implications really hit home.

There is explicit racialization of crime in San Antonio. The imaginary of an undocumented immigrant who is dangerous appears in most of our interviews with residents. The context of living where a predominance of people working—construction workers, domestic workers, security guards, maintenance workers, and others—are Spanish-speaking immigrants from Mexico and Central America often contributed to their fear talk.

Gated communities are a form of security capitalism that is dependent on the segregation of spaces, and in this case these separations are racialized. In the interviews completed on suburban Long Island, few residents make overtly racist statements but talk about "changes" in their previous neighborhoods or say they were looking for a "nice" neighborhood with "nice" people. By contrast, many of the interviewees in San Antonio did not hesitate to discuss their racial views, while at the same time protesting that they were not bigots.

These discursive strategies reflect the often racist foundations of living in a gated community and the historical use of exclusionary governance strategies when deed restrictions were deemed illegal in 1948. Homeowners' associations (HOAs), common interest developments (CIDs), condominiums, and some forms of cooperative housing grew out of urban planners and real estate agents working together to restrict purchases by race, class, and ethnicity.[5] The racist underpinning of securitization in the United States is generally recognized, but we argue that these same prejudices drive securitization measures worldwide. Racist undercurrents drive much of the motivation for living in a gated community, rationalized as fear and anxiety.

Gated communities continue to grow in the western, southwestern, and southern sections of the US. The last housing census that identified "secured communities" reported 11 million units/households in 2015, up from an estimated 10 million in 2010, 7 million in 2001, and an estimated 3 million units in 20,000 gated communities in 1997.[6] Changes in the household survey and conflicting definitions of *secured* make it difficult to interpret this increase accurately. Another way to think about this growth is to consider that there were approximately five gated communities on Long Island in 1996 based on our fieldwork, while a 2022 real estate advertisement for gated communities on Long Island listed forty, an eightfold increase. While cities tend to have fewer gated communities, high walls and alarmed or ID card–activated gates are being added to apartment and townhouse complexes giving them a citadel-like appearance. New forms of gating are also appearing, such as at the Reserve in North Carolina, where wealthy buyers can purchase homes in low-density gated communities that offer large house lots of 10 to 44.5 acres with monthly fees of $2,000 to $3,000 to cover the private roads, security gates, and cameras. Strict architectural guidelines maintain the "woodsy" feel of the area.[7]

Research on the social distance between gated communities and the surrounding neighborhoods in southwestern US metropolitan areas indicates that enclosed communities contribute significantly to segregated residential patterns. Researchers found statistically significant segregation between white and Hispanic residents and uncovered age segregation based on the large number of retirement communities. While there is increased heterogeneity and spatial diffusion of Hispanics, Asians, and other minorities in the region, gated communities aggregate this diversity into socioeconomically and racially homogeneous enclaves.[8]

The growing supply of and demand for these private developments is based on emotional, social, and financial motives. Saturation of the home environment with fear and insecurity combined with anxieties about investment value, mounting debt, and job insecurity interact with the profitability of the private housing developments for construction companies and local governments.

Economic and social forces intensified by a national climate of growing inequality, unending war, and militarization of everyday life as well imaginaries of lurking terrorists and illegal immigrants are exploited by the media creating a culture of fear, that is discussed further in later chapters of this book.

Yet, some causes are not directly related to fear, anxiety, or even securitization but reflect current economic trends and public service needs. Local municipalities on Long Island and new San Antonio suburbs are strapped for money and do not have the resources to construct new housing—or highway spurs, feeder roads, and service infrastructure—to bolster the tax base. A large, growing city like San Antonio is constantly falling behind in providing even basic municipal services, much less installing electric lines, water sewers, or paving. Small townships on Long Island face the same problems and are unable to support residential growth to attract businesses and commercial centers.

Private developers look for opportunities to make advantageous deals with local townships or municipalities that offer greater zoning density in exchange for putting in housing with basic services and physical infrastructure. The developer produces a master plan and an architectural and landscape design to submit to the local authorities. Once approved, the developer builds the proposed project, including streets, lights, water, landscaping, and other services, often working with various local and national vendors.

Rather than constructing an open neighborhood like the surrounding area, these private developments utilize walls, fences, and a variety of identity-recognition gates that restrict entrance and access. Amenities such as walking paths, swimming pools, tennis courts, or landscaped green space are enjoyed only by those who live there. Buyer demand for this kind of fortress security, high level of amenities, and new construction draws interested residents, while the town or city benefits from a broader, middle- and upper-middle-class tax base without any financial investment, taking on debt, or responsibility for maintenance of the infrastructure.

The resulting gated communities, however, change the social relations, sense of security, and political subjectivity of the residents who decide that their fears and concerns warrant the extra expense of the initial purchase or rental fee. As discussed, a variety of fears draw them, but other aspects of the lifestyle influence their future decision-making. Gated community residents say that once they have lived in a secured environment, they would never live outside one. This sentiment was widely reported regardless of whether they live on Long Island or in suburban San Antonio. Other researchers studying gated communities in India, Egypt, Argentina, and South Africa find the same sentiment, even though the crime rates vary dramatically—from low in the US to very high in South Africa and Mexico. The crime rate and level of fear are not correlated. In places with high crime, as documented by the police and other authorities, the expression of fear is the same as in areas such as suburban San Antonio and Long Island where there are much lower levels of crime.

These securitization practices, however, tend to shape a particular kind of resident and set of social relationships that are reproduced and impact society at large. It is not just the gates, walls, and guards that do the work of "securitizing" and reducing fear, because the fears and anxieties are embedded in many aspects of contemporary urban and suburban life. What gating offers that is so addictive and reassuring is the many levels of security produced through an interlocking system of controls that are formidable. Further, the levels of security include not simply the security apparatus to protect residents from harm, but control of everyday behavior to insure greater predictability of the social and physical environment. It becomes effortless to discriminate and employ exclusionary practices even for residents who are opposed to explicit social segregation. Thus, residents do not need to confront the implications of walling off and surveilling others to create a fortress that protects only them.

Many gated community residents protest that they are not racist, but are making their homes safe for their children, have moved because they were robbed, or found their previous neighborhood dirty or noisy. They just want a "nice" community with "nice" people and anticipate that a gated community will guarantee what they are looking for.

Not surprisingly, gated community residents are not necessarily aware that they are seen by people outside the walls as living in an elite and exclusionary place, even if modest in amenities and design. But while residents said they feel safer knowing they are protected; it also increases their anxiety about "someone getting in" as an everyday occurrence. Driving in and out of the gate or talking to the guards—sometimes even surveilling the guards to see if they are doing their job—generates an atmosphere of worry reinforced by the material environment. "What am I going to do if the guards don't do a good job?" an interviewee asks us. "I depend on them for my safety." Although one answer is to call a neighbor, the structure of governance often harms the neighborliness in many of the gated communities we worked in. As more residents depend on the homeowners' association board to manage community relations, the fewer relationships residents develop. Thus, only a small fraction of interviewees say they have friends or close neighbors living nearby.

The securitization of gated communities depends on producing a "nice," clean space that is physically delimited by enclosure and surveilled by guards, cameras, and residents. Some gated communities have a neighborhood watch or hire private guards who roam the neighborhood, checking on homes throughout the night. Residents tend to be economically homogeneous based on the cost of homes and the financial requirements of the application imposed by a homeowners', condominium, or cooperative board. With this kind of homogeneity and the resulting whiteness, the community becomes racialized, where racial and ethnic difference is highlighted. Guards and neighbors identify other residents as "people like us," and the moment that someone appears who is different, they are considered suspect. The chilling case of Trayvon Martin presented in the Introduction illustrates how the racialization of space works to create a secure environment for those who belong, but is dangerous, even violent, for "others." The case illuminates the power of racialized space to identify a "suspicious" outsider by gender, race and age.

Most gated communities are organized as condominiums with homeowners' associations. Buyers purchase their property fee simple, but collectively own the infrastructure (lighting, water, sewer, trash pickup), amenities (pool, clubhouse, tennis courts), and landscape (plants, lawns, pathways, ponds, and flowers) that are maintained and improved by monthly fees and additional yearly assessments. The board is responsible for guaranteeing that prospective buyers have the financial and job stability to obtain a mortgage and pay the fees since the community carries the additional burden if a member defaults. The constitution and functioning of the board thus further secure the environment by restricting the pool of potential purchasers to those with the essential credentials. The review of prospective buyers' financials includes an assessment of their occupational history (usually five years of tax returns and references) and social acceptability (based on letters from clubs, other associations, corporate relationships, and friends). This financial and class-based screening is dictated by the governing documents and legal requirements of incorporation.

Thus, gated communities are securitized by various layers of power—including fear of violence—and architectural and financial control. Securitization begins with spatial enclosure, marked borders, and physical barriers that limit who enters. Once the perimeter is secured, like a war zone, the social and racial purification of space occurs based on who can purchase or rent a home, get a mortgage, or pass the financial review. These restrictions are often referred to as "laissez-faire" racism, that is, how financialization processes and credential reviews select for white and middle- to upper-middle-class residents. As the costs of housing and financing increase, the more elite the community becomes.

When a neighborhood becomes more homogeneous and purified, surveillance strategies can easily focus on "nonresidents" and "those who don't belong." Surveillance of an enclosed space intensifies the sense of interiority that is produced and then defended. Private governance with an elected or appointed board controls community decision-making, adding a layer of rules and regulations (the so-called CC&Rs) that control the behavior of residents (did you put out your trash can on time? did you pick up after your dog?) and minimize variations in the landscape design and plantings (color of house paint that can be used, no flowers in the front yard). Architectural guidelines and a limited palette of neutral colors ensure a particular aesthetic look, reinforcing an elite taste culture that attracts buyers who want to live in an upper-middle-class or elite environment. The layering of security apparatus—physical enclosure, surveillance strategies, financial restrictions, and aesthetic choices—provides the desired security that residents are seeking and isolates them from the perceived ills and risks of a democratic society.

Wendy Brown argues that the irony of late modernity is that the walling meant to "mark and enforce an inside/outside distinction—a boundary between 'us' and 'them' and between friend and enemy" erodes these distinctions.[9] The building of border walls—between the US and Mexico, Israel and Palestine—actually signals the fragility of national boundaries and weakening of sovereign state power.

Taking her lead, it seems that the psychological, social, and physical interiority of gating reflects the weakening of middle-class dominance due to its vulnerability in the face of economic restructuring and deindustrialization in a rapidly globalizing world. The fixtures of the American dream—a mortgaged house, a car, good schools, vacations, and leisure, all supported by a well-paid and secure job—are increasing difficult to obtain much less maintain. The life, liberty, and pursuit of happiness in the American imagination based on owning a house appreciating in value and living a middle-class family lifestyle is fading with neoliberal policies, fewer social supports, and more frequent economic downturns. The mantra of life, security, and the pursuit of individual success is more appropriate.

Gated communities, and private urban developments such as Hudson Yards, discussed in the next chapter, spatialize and then securitize risk in such a way that it falls disproportionately on those who live outside the "walls" or prestigious commercial property. The future can be glimpsed in the imaginary of splintered urbanism[10] where gated communities are connected to one another and to luxury restaurants and malls, bypassing the remaining inhabitants struggling to survive in informal settlements or on the streets. Setha vividly recalls spending time in Caracas living in a gated compound and riding in an armored car to a securitized mall for dinner. When she tried to go for a walk, she was told that it was not possible outside the guarded areas. When she asked her hosts if they found this life restrictive, they said that it was better than living with constant fear.

The solidarity of anxiety that forms among gated community residents further reinforces the social controls imposed by architecture, law, and spatial governance creating the chilling Foucauldian insight that they are trapped within a world of their own making. In dystopic novels[11] about gating and as well as in the nightmare of contemporary homelessness, everyone loses, and the moral fiber of society decays or worse becomes irrelevant.

Post-Foucauldian scholar Michalis Lianos observes that social control is now embedded everywhere by the consensual interaction of the user and the institution and regularized around invisible, yet ubiquitous threats.[12] This proposition accurately reflects the current dilemma of gating, that residents consent, indeed desire, the institutionalization of the HOA board with its rules and regulations, exclusionary admission processes, and excessive guarding and surveillance in the face of named and unnamed threats. But the consensual social controls do not extend outside the gated community, and gated community residents are not concerned about—much less aware of—the social and psychological violence imposed on those who are excluded. Gated communities and their residents are responding to invisible, and/or exaggerated, threats and defending themselves in multifarious ways without addressing the impact of their choices and way of life.

Walls do not merely protect but are productive of social relations that become fragmented, distanced, and intolerant and in some cases, violent and dangerous. Building gated communities is one way that the public sector, the town, or municipality gives up its responsibility for providing safety and services for all its residents, and instead divides and segregates residents by class, ethnicity and race, and age. As Brown asks, "When do the new walls become like the confining walls of a prison, rather than the comforting walls of a house? When does the fortress become a penitentiary?"[13]

It is this question that we must answer to combat the trend towards increasing numbers of secured residential enclaves. How do we convince people that the safety and security of gated communities is an illusion and that they already live in areas that have extremely low crime rates?

Why do these residents feel as if they are living in Mexico City or Johannesburg where people worry about the exact same things, yet the context is completely different?[14] What are they really afraid of? Is it a defense of white supremacy or a way to bolster a fragile middle-class identity? Social psychological and anthropological research reveals that people who are familiar with their neighbors feel safer and more secure. Social contact, and particularly meaningful engagement, lowers the fear of others, while driving back and forward each day stopping to wait for the guard (or electronic device) to lift a barrier or open a gate reiterates the fear that there is someone or something dangerous outside that is threatening.

Fear is a potent emotion as well as a political and social resource. It is a motivator of behavior and determines residential choices. Yet these choices are changing society and reconstructing the built environment in ways that are detrimental to democracy and belonging. There is no real protection from all forms of fear and anxiety, yet some people are determined that it can be purchased, regardless of the consequences. This securitized world is dependent on individuals wanting to escape imagined and real vulnerabilities.

CONCEPT NOTE: INTERIOR LIFE

Remember life under COVID-19 restrictions? Forbidden from meeting friends and neighbors in public spaces, living in a shrunken, indoor world of constant vigilance. We know that the social and psychological impact of this isolation was profound. Yet significant numbers of people elect to live in a permanent state of emergency, as if sociality is fundamentally dangerous, and walls must be built to keep disorder out. Today, around the world, many people aspire to live this kind of interior life.

A long line of conservative thinkers has explored the desire for a life under total control and constant security. For the wealthy, physical security and financial security are measured by physical privacy, and the availability of private services: private schools, clubs, resorts, and residences that are accessed by private entrances and exits, all patrolled by private security guards. The consequence is social isolation. Indeed, Ayn Rand closes *Atlas Shrugged* with her protagonists, the world's wealthiest innovators, abandoning society for a no-tax gated community in a secret Colorado valley. "We are not a state here, not a society of any kind," one of Rand's protagonists informs us, "We're just a voluntary association held together by nothing but every man's self-interest."[1]

The middle classes look sideways and up for glimpses of the people they aspire to be. There is always a higher level of exclusivity to aim for. An exclusive life is by definition one lived distant from others. And, the more distance one achieves, the more distinctive the interior world seems from the outside. But isolation from difference, including aspects of everyday life, narrows experience, and thus the imagination suffers, including the capacity to imagine the suffering and reality of others. Security never brings the peace it promises. Instead, it brings new strains of isolation and fear. The remedy, which is always more security, exacerbates those feelings.

How might we think about this security-fear dynamic in the contemporary moment? What architectural and social-structural form does it take? Elsewhere we have described the striation of the world with "security-scapes," from fortified public spaces and events to walled and watched private homes.[2] In *The World Interior of Capital*, philosopher Peter Sloterdijk offers the following vision of a world composed of securitized "crystal palaces":

> the interior . . . contains an elevator that transports residents to the five expansively constructed floors of relief . . . The first floor is for those who have succeeded

in partially or completely fulfilling the dream of income without performance; the second is frequented by an audience of relaxed citizens who profit from political security without themselves having any readiness to fight; the third is where those meet who participate in general provisions of immunity without having their own history of suffering; on the fourth, consumers of a knowledge whose acquisition requires no experience spread themselves out; and on the fifth one finds those who, through direct publication of their own person, have succeeded in becoming famous without presenting any achievement or publishing any work.[3]

The world Sloterdijk depicts resembles those depicted in dystopic science fiction, like the films *Zardoz* or *Elysium,* where a pampered elite live beneath protected domes.

The philosopher's work, and our own, points to the dialectic between withdrawal and securitization: people fleeing "chaos" in search of safety, but their withdrawal exacerbates the disorder—the higher the walls the more one needs additional security. These days, airports, hotels, shopping malls, and theme parks are not merely safe; they are secure, "clean" or "sterile" spaces that are free from the turmoil of everyday life. To free people from security, we must understand the dynamics at work, especially the fact that security capitalism is a poor substitute for public safety and social solidarity, because a life lived with others, no matter the risk, is always more satisfying than isolation in a fortress.

2 TAKE BACK THE CITY

Security as a Way of Life in New York City

Elaine, with her curly brown hair and navy striped T-shirt, looks much younger than her age. She runs every day before going to work as a manager of a children's magazine and cooks healthy dinners for her husband, dog, and sometimes a visiting son or grandson. A member of a book club, a neighborhood bridge group, and frequently a student in New York University's adult online classes, she has lived in New York City since her first job as a bookkeeper at eighteen. She loves to shop, see friends, attend plays, and meet new people by giving parties and holiday gatherings. The fast pace and variety of Manhattan enables a lifestyle that offers a pleasant range of choices in her activities and social settings, with the side benefit of not having to travel far from home.

But her enjoyment of the city has been marred, she says, by the increasing number of homeless people on the streets and rising crime rates during the COVID-19 pandemic, personal intrusions that remind her of the 1980s when she lived near Tompkins Square Park. Back then, the streets were full of panhandlers, the park poorly maintained with a growing tent encampment, and she became afraid to go out alone at night because of purse-snatching and muggings.

Elaine was ecstatic after her first visit to Hudson Yards, a new kind of civic space that opened shortly before the arrival of COVID-19. The high-end shopping mall, trendy restaurants, a city-sponsored cultural center for art and theater—The Shed—and a five-acre public square flank the centerpiece, the "Vessel," a 16-story, 150-foot-tall sculpture by Thomas Heatherwick. This central area is part of the largest private real-estate development in US history projected to cost $25 billion, comprising seventeen million square feet of commercial, residential, and civic space.[1]

Built on columns constructed by the MTA in the early 1970s over the Pennsylvania Station railyards and stretching from 30th to 34th Streets between 10th and 12th Avenues, Related Companies and Oxford Properties Group were awarded the MTA contract in 2008 and invested $400 million (now $1 billion) to complete the platform. The first fifty-two-story office tower, 10 Hudson Yards, straddling the well-beloved High Line, broke ground in 2010, and by 2019 the first section of what is planned to be sixteen buildings—including a school, parkland, and apartments—was in place.[2] Of the fourteen acres of public open space, much of it ended up being a fancy drive-through and drop-off area for the mall and restaurants.

The remaining open area is encroached upon by a large semipermanent structure managed by Equinox and pop-up buildings for selling expensive watches and technology devices. Café chairs and tables for purchasing coffee and snacks extend into the space from restaurants located in the shopping mall.[3]

Elaine's description of her initial visit included the available valet parking if she wanted to drive, but also the brand-new subway stop—a station with the reassuring presence of transit police and surveillance cameras. The subway stop and Hudson Yards are conveniently linked by a bridge to the High Line, allowing a pleasant hike from 34th to 12th Street on a landscaped walkway above the noise and traffic. On the north side of the public

Figure 1. The Railyards at Hudson Yards. Photograph by Setha Low

Figure 2. Backyard at Hudson Yards. Photograph by Troy Simpson

space, Soul Cycle classes are offered in a tent, while the central area is filled by the "Back Porch," with rows of beach chairs facing a large movie screen ready to be individually rented by scanning the Wells Fargo code on an attached card.

A restaurant is situated on the southern edge of the public area, with a bar and striking views of the Hudson River. Narrow gravel paths and a long, continuous bench rims the area with multiple surveillance cameras visibly encircling the site. If you are disoriented by all of this, Elaine adds, nearby kiosks advertising events and sales can help locate where you want to go, while a tiny built-in camera records your query as part of its smart city design to improve consumer experience.

"We are creating a museum of architecture and a whole new way of life," according to Stephen Ross, the president of Related[4] and Elaine agrees with him.

The Vessel is a major draw during Elaine's early visits as a place to bring friends, to take an Instagram picture, and for the spectacular views of the city. Gaining entrance required signing a form that gave Related the rights to any photographs or social media posts taken, and private guards made sure that everyone signed before proceeding up the long and winding staircase. But after four tragic suicides from the wide-open structure—the most recent being a fourteen-year-old boy in July 2021—the Vessel was permanently closed.

Elaine's husband, Herbert, who sports a grey crew cut and enjoys wearing jeans when not at work, thinks Hudson Yards is a great solution for reviving what was a deteriorated and difficult-to-build-on part of the city. Trained as an engineer with experience working on construction projects in Florida, he wonders about the developer's ability to finance the surrounding corporate office towers and condominiums—as well as the school and affordable apartments—still to be built. Neiman-Marcus, the mall's anchor store, planned to relocate its corporate headquarters but had already pulled out by 2020. Ninety percent of the offices are transfers from Midtown rather than new tenants (for example, the Time Warner Center moved from Columbus Circle), and residential sales have been slow with 50 percent of the units at 35 Hudson Yards still empty.[5]

Herbert has had plenty of experience with failed projects that left the construction company and investors with uncollectable losses and bank debt, and the city without anticipated real estate taxes and other forms of revenue. Regardless of the financial risks, however, he

Figure 3. The Vessel and Plaza at Hudson Yards. Photograph by Taryn Fivek

thought the masterminds of the project had done a good job attracting capital investment to an underutilized neighborhood, a strategy that would bring the "right kind of people" and revitalize the area.

Aided by the NYC 2012 plan, a pro-business corporate model of leadership did what was needed by covering over the below-grade railroad tracks to create a lively tourist and commercial center. While the city offered deep tax cuts and leased the property rights in such a way that might not benefit the city for years, the strategy was thought to be critical to attracting global companies as well as international visitors who wanted a compelling residential real estate investment.

"What else might the city have done with the site?" Herbert speculated.

When asked about the numerous guards, uniformed staff, visible and invisible surveillance systems, and physical barriers, Elaine responded that without private security services, controlled entrances, and AI face-recognition cameras, she might not feel as comfortable in such a large urban complex.

Herbert's take on the amount of private seating, expensive cycling classes, lack of open walkways, and benches in the last public space of any size in Manhattan was to view the idea of Hudson Yards as more about branding Manhattan as the luxury city, a strategy begun by Mayor Bloomberg and supported by the finance and real estate industries. This mixed-use development is only one piece of an overall plan to enhance quality public space that appeals to international elites and corporations so they will continue to invest and live in the city.

Another perspective on Hudson Yards is offered by Madeleine—a young, single news producer, who goes to the mall to shop for high-quality workout clothes. She is impressed with the lack of crowds and the array of specialty athletic clothing stores, such as Lululemon and Athletica—a seamless shopping experience that includes easy transportation, gourmet coffee shops, and the "right" kinds of stores all in one place.

When she came to try the restaurants one evening, Madeleine adds that she felt "totally safe" walking the area as she waited for friends. The private guards in black uniforms scattered around reassured her just by their presence. "It's a nice place," she said to her friends, "comfortable and so upscale." The expanse of curved glass, towering steel columns, unusual architecture, and mall lighting made it feel special even in New York City. "Everything you want is at your doorstep."

Public spaces dedicated to providing a safe, secure, clean, and—especially in the case of Hudson Yards—"upscale" urban experience reflect a critical aspect of security capitalism, one that draws upon multiple meanings of "being secure" for middle-class visitors and city investors.[6] In the previous chapter, security emerges as a personal concern about one's safety based on racialized fear of others. Security at Hudson Yards is more about maintaining class status and relative standing by controlling the built area for a "perfect," frictionless social experience, and securitizing the built environment through financialization practices. Viewed from this perspective, "feeling safe and secure" centers on anxiety about encountering certain people whose presence might otherwise threaten or diminish their image of themselves as upper-middle-class users or interfere with the desired "elite" experience conveyed by the site.

Securitization refers to a nexus of (1) individuals searching for safety within an insecure state, (2) state militarization and production of fearful citizens, and (3) the financial securitization of mortgages and other monetary instruments to reduce financial risk. These processes contribute to—and in some cases even determine—the insidious array of physical, moral, and legal environments that enable displacement and immobility that differentially impact people and communities.

Even though securitization is driven by fear—fear of others and fear of economic failure, and in this sense is a defensive strategy, it constrains the circulation and occupation of space by others. By securitizing environments of the middle and upper-middle classes through walling off and strategies of everyday financialization, immigrants, working-class, and poorer people find it difficult to enter and stay in these public spaces. Such geographic exclusionary practices have a greater impact than just creating a secure neighborhood, and instead produce a landscape of physical and psychological barriers and class-inflected boundaries that enclose those within, all the while impeding the mobility and access of those outside.

When examining this type of urban fabric, it's useful to think about security at different scales, moving away from the national security focus (though still important in any city during an event such as 9/11) and understand the multiple layers of fear and anxiety produced and experienced in the historical and political context of New York City. Elaine, Herbert, and Madeleine want to be secure in a way that their bodies and senses will not be threatened—either directly through being the victim of a crime or violence, or indirectly by encountering the types of people they tend to associate with crime and other-ness.[7] This incipient fear of others has created opportunities for generating a politics of fear—a dominant motif driving certain cable news media organizations and elements of popular culture—that focuses attention almost exclusively on reporting crime characterized by victimization narratives that are racialized, gendered, and classed.[8]

Even though relevant data show that New York City is currently safer than at any previous time, fear remains a central focus of everyday discourse, abetted by the repetition of media reports of assaults and murders that make it seem as if a crime wave is rampant; it follows that the predictable result is a self-reinforcing normalization of such stoked fears. Middle-class New Yorkers, then, often find it hard to believe the statistics regarding actual crime rates rather than their own media-conditioned perceptions of "how things really are" at the street level.

Perceptions that influence a sense of fear and anxiety—whether reality-based or not—consistently reinforce a desire for controlled built environments with visible evidence of policing and surveillance.

Arguably, security from physical harm and victimization should be a right enjoyed by all New Yorkers. But the fear of others—especially when combined with a politics of fear—produces a situation where the security of the middle class limits the use of urban space by poorer and more marginalized individuals. An elaborate security apparatus ensures that certain "others" are not visible or encountered, in effect excluding them by default from the commonly shared space.

Consider, too, the fraught tradition in the United States of conditioning citizens to be anxious and fearful. Masco attributes a marked increase in this behavior to the Cold War, when children were directed to hide under school desks as a drill, and many families dug bomb shelters in their backyards to protect themselves from the threat of a nuclear attack.[9] An emergent collective sentiment and the creation of an apprehensive affective atmosphere thus became permanent attributes of American life, manipulated by self-interested elements of the security state to increase public acceptance (and docility) about the risks of external threats.

Fear took on a more racialized character during 1950s and 1960s. White flight to New York City's suburbs in the face of increasing numbers of Black and Hispanic/Latino residents intensified existing racial and social segregation. Downward mobility due to deindustrialization and the loss of jobs threatened the well-being of the working and middle classes, prompting a sense of competition with the newcomers, the ones who were purportedly taking "our" jobs. The later transition to a service economy further restructured existing class structures and endangered the comfortable and economically "secure" lifestyle of many New York City families. The increasing surveillance load and policing of people of color was thereby rationalized as a necessary measure to secure the streets.

Predictably, the terrorist attack on the World Trade Center on September 11, 2001 (9/11), reawakened the dormant sense of Cold War–era fear and anxiety, though this time arising from a merciless foreign enemy with different faces and culture. Combat troops in full battle gear were assigned to every public space and transportation hub, accompanied by the reinstatement of stop-and-frisk policing, restrictions on air travel, selective immigration limits, and mandatory photo-ID registration to enter office buildings, unavoidable daily reminders of the looming risks of terrorism to personal safety.

9/11 accelerated the securitization of public space, hardening security measures and increasing technologically advanced security systems alongside the private restrictions already in place. Police officers and canine security that protected privately owned public spaces in the 1990s were replaced by monitored live-streaming video cameras; and public spaces were flooded with signs to be vigilant about strangers, unattended packages, and people acting "suspiciously." Racial profiling increased, often targeting persons who were perceived to be Muslims, and though not themselves Muslim, members of the Sikh community were sometimes targeted because their traditional turbans aroused suspicion. An amorphous blend of Islamophobia seemed to grip a once tolerant city. Privatization efforts that were earlier credited with "saving" public spaces became one of the only means for generating new public space, and places that were already privatized became even more securitized during this chaotic period.

Russian President Vladimir Putin's threats to use nuclear weapons to gain control of Ukraine in 2022 further revitalized Cold War anxieties, a tactic that many observers interpreted as a deliberate weaponization of fear, fueling a climate of uncertainty. Authoritarian governments, it would seem, are especially skilled at playing the ultimate card in the perverse game of threatening everyone's security.

The final impetus for securitizing public space was the sweeping impact of the COVID-19 pandemic. During its height, public spaces became critical resources for satisfying the most basic social, cultural, psychological, economic, and health needs, but only some people had unfettered access to safe and secure spaces. Lower income areas had few open green spaces and struggled with overfilled streets due to the density of housing and crowded apartments that offered little respite from being shut inside.

The inequality in access to public space was apparent in everything from higher rates of disease to the lack of places for children to play. Some wealthier families reportedly left the city and only came back when the worst of the pandemic was over. Homelessness grew to 60,000 people and many "undomiciled" persons slept in the subways, afraid of the potentially contagious conditions in the city's shelters. Using face masks (or not) became symbolic of one's political identity. The term *social distancing*, rather than the more accurate *physical distancing*, to reduce transmission of the virus, became an apt (if unintended) metaphor describing this fraught period.

With each of these transitions in the objects of fear and anxiety—perceptions of crime and unsafe streets, international tensions, threats of terrorist attacks, and the raging COVID-19 pandemic—the interests of security capitalism thrived. Those with financial means demanded more controlled public spaces and urban infrastructure if they were going to stay in the city, and the pandemic illustrated just how easy it was for the upper and professional classes to self-isolate and leave the city once they were able to work from home. At the same time, the pandemic highlighted the dangers of relying on the healthcare, service, and hospitality sectors for economic viability; in fact, the closing of most restaurants, hotels, small stores, and coffee shops—the mainstay of the lower end of New York City's job-based economy—was a stark reminder of the vulnerability of such face-to-face jobs. While it is difficult to pry apart all the factors shaping the new privatized public landscape, the securitization of a place like Hudson Yards appears overdetermined.

While a desire for a secure city includes freedom from crime and assaults for some, and the ability to buy "security" when you live in or even visit a place like Hudson Yards, the idea also encompasses the financial security of the city and the real estate investments that ensure solvency. New York City has always been in competition with other cities to attract talent, residents, and (most importantly) investors to maintain financial viability. Ever since the 1970s, when New York City underwent a fiscal crisis, unease that it could happen again influences every municipal decision, especially those affecting finance, insurance, and real estate(FIRE), the core industries of the city's wealth and economic stability.[10] Economic-financial security generally relies on a predictable and stable political system, but since 9/11, it increasingly relies on an urban militarism that protects investments in real estate development, leveraged bonds and mortgages, and new instruments of financialization.[11]

Underlying the attempt to produce a new type of securitized built environment was the combination of a dwindling municipal tax base, the loss of small industries and factories that provided a middle-class wage, the skyrocketing cost of living and renting due to real estate and finance speculation, and residents haunted by the memory of the bankruptcy, physical deterioration, and high crime rate of noir New York City in the 1970s. Digging out of the economic, psychological, and social impact of those years strained the public sector's capacity to maintain its infrastructure, especially public spaces, many of which became derelict and dangerous. Bryant Park at 42nd Street, today a model urban space, was then full of drugs and dealers, a place one usually adventurous academic researcher scurried past when the Graduate Center of the City University of New York was located across the street. This historical reality is inscribed in the collective memory of many city residents—a frightful image that continues to have potency today. It can also be understood as a lingering sequela of that era, one that functions to propel Manhattan, and recently parts of Brooklyn, into designing increasingly gentrified, white, middle-class public spaces.

New York City is by no means alone in the quest for economic security with stable home prices and rents, good paying jobs, and an endless selection of cultural and entertainment attractions. It competes with other major cities to maintain a reputation as a safe investment with high real estate values and a portfolio of amenities. Yet the underlying impetus—certainly the proffered reasoning—for privatizing public space and securitizing the streets for the middle and elite classes is to save the city from another period of decline and insolvency.

The irony is that many aspects of the privatization of public space that dominate places like Hudson Yards evolved from grassroots community-based efforts begun in the 1970s. The challenge of "taking back the city" meant reclaiming abandoned and unmaintained public city property by neighborhood groups. Cleaning up littered and neglected lots—then starting community gardens or managing rundown parks through "friends of the park" groups—formed the backbone of residential cohesion. These groups also generated new public/private relationships and business associations to manage public spaces that became more powerful and sophisticated over time.

Frustrated city residents took over dilapidated parks deserted by the eviscerated Department of Parks and Recreation, often planting flowers, pruning trees, and repairing playground equipment.[12] Volunteers created a shadow Parks Department, taking over the daily maintenance, while preservationists and residents of nearby brownstones formed action groups —Friends of Prospect Park, Save Central Park Committee, and Friends of Fort Greene Park—aimed at saving trees and stopping the demolition of historic buildings. These groups eventually became institutionalized as park conservancies—Central Park Conservancy was the first in 1980—paying administrators and raising most of the operating budget, privatizing park management, and professionalizing decision-making. While the results were often dramatic, most of the positive outcomes occurred in wealthier neighborhoods with available leadership and funding.

Business improvement districts (BIDs), such as the 42nd Street Partnership, were another strategy for privatizing the cleaning and monitoring of sidewalks and streets. BIDs developed initially to enhance the public environment—the streetscape, lighting, signage, and sidewalks—as well as to decrease vandalism and crime due to urban disinvestment in the 1970s and 1980s. Business associations were formed with the power to tax local commercial enterprises as a means of generating adequate funds for neighborhood improvements in cooperation with the city. The idea was to treat aggregated commercial spaces as marketable commodities and pursue place-based and branding activities through advertising and promotional campaigns. BIDs tapped into the "creativity" and "coolness" of the city to attract younger middle-class consumers, instituting street maintenance and security programs with uniformed workers and community ambassadors to improve their image as "clean, safe and friendly" places to live and work.[13]

Privately owned public spaces (POPS) were created in New York City by a 1961 law that permitted developers additional floor space and building height in exchange for constructing public pocket-parks, mid-block gardens, and corporate plazas as part of their projects. A variety of new public/private arrangements and corporate-sponsored POPS were designed, but many remained vacant and unused. A 2000 study by Gerald Kayden found that a majority of New York City's 550 privately owned public spaces had features that deterred people from entering or staying.[14] Jeremy Nemeth studied 163 spaces and found that POPS had deleterious effects on citizenship and representation,[15] while Smithsimon found that POPS were intentionally designed to be exclusionary.[16] By December

2022, New York City Department of Buildings inspections found that one in five of the current 598 POPS properties violated their agreements to remain open and accessible.[17] Violations include POPS filled with businesses and construction materials or restricted by padlocked gates and hostile architecture.[18] Regardless of these findings POPS, BIDs, public/private conservancies, limited partnerships, and other kinds of public/private governance structures have become global models for how to produce well-maintained and monitored public spaces.

But while these interventions improve physical conditions in select areas, they do little to improve the funding for parts of the city that lack a sufficient nexus of private businesses or engaged citizens with the resources to support them. Public funding for such efforts, always scarce, continues to decline, ensuring increased dependence on private support for public goods, including any expansion or improvement of public space. This array of public/private partnerships—varying from public spaces governed privately, to private spaces that are supposedly public but are not welcoming or accessible—form the groundwork for the kinds of public spaces considered possible or desirable in post–fiscal crisis New York City.

Regardless of the scale of intervention, security divides and fragments urban space.[19] In his discussion of counterterrorism in Nairobi, Zoltan Gluck employs the term "security urbanism"[20] to characterize how the city is coded by zones of safety and danger. Beirut is also transformed by hierarchies of urban space segregated by religious and ethnic factions, with unequal repercussions for differently situated city dwellers.[21] In New York the motive for these "security zones" is not counterterrorism or religious/ethnic warfare, but protection of capital investment. Rather than security urbanism, then, we argue that the built environment of New York City is organized by security capitalism.

To learn more about Hudson Yards, Setha attended presentations by researchers currently studying the site. Taryn Fivek's project focuses on the financialization of Hudson Yards and strategies for generating funds such as raising $1.2 billion by selling 10,000 EB-5 visas to potential investors.[22] A total of approximately $9 billion in reduced taxes, abatements, and the construction of new public infrastructure like the new subway station contributes to the profitability for buyers and developers. Even though Hudson Yards has not yet turned a profit, a tax abatement on the purchase of a $23 million condominium is a considerable financial incentive for the very rich. The completed towers remain partially empty, and the upper floors of the mall deserted. To make up for these losses, Related Companies auctioned off portions of their ground lease to a restaurant and other vendors. The most recent idea to increase cash flow is to open a casino.

Fivek concludes that while Hudson Yards privileges the wealthiest of residents, it is in one of the most socioeconomically unequal areas of the city with Section 8 housing residents whose needs are not being addressed even though the plan was politically and economically supported by the city. Her findings confirm my interviews and archival research that the financial objectives of Hudson Yards are dependent on attracting global capital and investment by wealthy individuals and that the city underwrote this endeavor with preferential tax treatment and new infrastructure. To date it is unclear whether the city's investment will pay off, and if so, when.

Troy Simpson has been studying the evolution and use of the central public space in Hudson Yards for the past two years.[23] His ethnographic study focuses on the use of the space, its "smart" attributes, and how visitors react to different behavioral settings by interviewing visitors and the designers, documenting user activities and movements, and analyzing the ways that the site's publicness is controlled.

Simpson finds that there are exclusive use areas, such as the Backyard and Soul Cycle, that require fees to enter. Provisional seating at tables and chairs set in the gravel areas are popular but disappeared one Saturday. There are roped-off areas that limit access to some of the benches and open space, and the pathways are narrow in comparison to the gravel areas that are difficult to walk in. A code of conduct is prominently displayed listing all the prohibited activities—including lying down or obstructing the sitting areas, active sports such as skateboarding or rollerblading, drinking alcohol, barbecuing, playing amplified music, or letting dogs off-leash. Much of the seating uses brass-colored bollards with lights to demarcate the café tables and entrances of the rest of the space.

In some public areas the rules of use are very explicit, such as the controlled access to the Vessel guarded by men in black, sign-in sheets, restrictions on photographing, and the need to present tickets that were processed only online when it was previously open. But in other areas the provision of amenities is ambiguous, without clear signage announcing whether the space is for (or not for) public use. The resulting landscape cannot be read and at times leaves visitors with a sense of ambivalence about being welcome. There is a palpable feeling that this is a place for people with money that makes relaxing feel transgressive, but also enticing. Hudson Yards radiates a seductive allure of what it might be like to be one of the elite, yet also reminds visitors who do not belong that their status is temporary.[24] Some interviewees comment directly on the affective atmosphere of behavioral control and how the cost of activities makes it feel exclusive.

> *I think like I said about the mall, honestly, if you look at the Vessel, as well, it has a very, I don't know, I'm feeling a very pervasive atmosphere of how I should behave. Like, I would never put a blanket down and like have a picnic or treat this space in a terribly comfortable way. Like, I feel awkward just even sitting here, almost. I feel like I need to, I don't know the space is just a little, and this isn't the correct word for it, but it feels a little bougie. Um, yeah, I feel a little out of place here.*

I'm a retiree. Who can afford what they are selling here? . . . This my first time here. I like the view from up there. And it's good they have done something with it because it was sitting here dilapidated. People will be employed, and tourists will be buying the Fendi and whatever, generating more money. Not for us, really, in terms of spending. We brought our lunch.[25]

Simpson concludes that Hudson Yards offers behavioral settings through exclusive use, rule setting, and ambiguous provision of amenities that create a class-based environment where people "perform" wealth whether they are wealthy or not. His analysis resonates with our view that this urban development is part of a class-based strategy to take back the city for the middle class as part of Bloomberg's goal of branding New York as a luxury city.[26] Hudson Yards represents a new image of New York, with a secure, new, clean, "high-class" style that visitors and residents who identify with this representation love. As a visitor puts it:

I mean, there's . . . tons of people coming here to take pictures to show everybody else a style, I guess. You know, they're going to post it on Instagram or whatnot to say, "Oh yeah, look at how great New York looks, and look at how great I look in New York." Like, especially some of the backdrops you can have here, it's incredibly new and clean. And if that's what you're going for with your own style, then it's perfect.[27]

Fear and anxiety, from whatever source, create a desire for security that begins at the level of the body—protection from physical and psychological harm—and scales up through the securitization of the home, neighborhood, city, and nation. People want solutions to their perceived insecurity and vulnerability; thus, material and technological infrastructures are put in place—from surveillance and policing systems to military personnel and technologies. These infrastructures create opportunities for accumulating capital and offer new sources of profit. The producers of security infrastructures—from transnational corporations to municipal services and private security companies—reinforce perceptions of threats and the need for risk assessment and caution through the media, built environment, and imagined dystopias. As these infrastructures and technologies multiply, they have a physical impact and other effects that remind people of their fears and dependence on infrastructure for protection. Fear of others and the politics of fear change social relations in permanent ways, replacing previously accepted norms and rules of society.

Thus, our oftentimes irrational history of national insecurity, personal anxiety, city bankruptcy, and racialized fearmongering provides a worrisome background for the underlying threats and imaginings that are symbolically and materially condensed in urban security-scapes like Hudson Yards. By design and intent, security-scapes promote a form of ambient power, materially constituted by surveillance cameras, barriers and bollards, private guards, and police officers, eliciting a fear-filled atmosphere even when adorned with the trappings of pleasure, affluence, and tranquility.[28]

While Hudson Yard's security apparatus subtly reminds visitors of their vulnerability, it also reassures them that they will be kept safe, physically, and socially, for the price of admission. This commodification of fear—that is, the promotional culture that urges us to protect ourselves against the threat of unknown risk or imagined harm—offers the opportunity to purchase physical, economic, and class security at Hudson Yards through one-stop shopping.[29] Comparable to the rise of "luxury surveillance" offered by Amazon's suite of products, protection is purchased willingly, even though it draws upon the same tracking devices as Smart LINK that are forced on parolees or immigrants awaiting hearings.[30]

Thus, people such as Elaine, Herbert, and Madeleine, who love Hudson Yards, do not question why other New Yorkers, particularly minority residents and people of color are absent or invisible, unless they are workers in restaurants, shop clerks, or security guards. Increasingly New York middle-class society has become security-centered, run by the producers of security and those who benefit. "What's wrong," you think, "with a safe, clean, and secure environment?" The catch is that it is for only a small fraction of the eight million residents, and the financial and social costs make it impossible to reproduce the same level of security in other less wealthy and unprofitable parts of the city.

The infrastructures of security capitalism metastasize, corrupting other forms of social relations, and prevent alternative remedies. But we are not simply pointing a finger at politicians and tech companies, or the transnational capitalist class, but implicating the middle-class and wealthy residents who contribute to this inequality. By seeking quick-fix solutions, becoming comfortable with the segregation, militarized policing, and physical barriers, they ignore the underlying causes that allow for their privileged position.

Herbert initially asked, "What else might they have done with the site?" to which we offer this answer: Hudson Yards could have contributed to the financial growth and redevelopment of New York City and at the same time offered an accessible and welcoming public space, a diverse array of commercial establishments, and a mix of affordable and luxury housing if there was the political will and public demand for a socially just built environment. It could have been a place like Brooklyn Bridge Park that uses private development funds and condominium fees to create a public space with activities and access for everyone. Brooklyn Bridge Park still retains a team of managers who maintain the landscape, provide equipment for volleyball, basketball, and other sports, and call the police if there is a need. But there must be a commitment to an equitable, inclusive city where all residents belong and have a place regardless of their economic means, race, ethnicity, immigrant status, sexual orientation, ability, and gender.

CONCEPT NOTE: SECURITY CAPITALISM

Around the world, people are choosing an interior life ringed by security. From New York to Nairobi, the wealthy—the social class that journalist Peggy Noonan calls "the protected"—are paying for illusory safety. They will say that they have little choice. Without security, they cannot sleep at night or get to work the following day; they cannot find peace of mind. For the protected, security is the infrastructure that supports their way of life. The more they live well, the less they wish to live like those who cannot afford security. However, no matter how high the walls are, absolute security remains elusive because walls only increase social distance and deepen divisions. The world outside the safe interior looks chaotic. It is worth remembering that the ancient Romans believed that security, *securitas*, was a state of mind, a lack of concern for things beyond one's control.

In its modern usage, *security* has several meanings, such as guaranteeing an obligation, safety from danger, or liberty understood as freedom from fear. The word originates in Old French, and *la sécurité* conveys the above meanings. *Capitalism* is an equally popular yet elusive term. In nineteenth-century France, *capitalisme* denoted the financing of war and defense. Historically and conceptually, then, security and capitalism are conjoined twins. Karl Marx tacitly understood this but focused on how security underpinned the bourgeois order by guaranteeing "the preservation of his person, his rights and his property." Security capitalism guarantees liberty, and liberty must be sacrificed to security. Thus, according to Marx, "the end appears as the means and the means as the end."[1]

Today, despite this being an era of low levels of homicide and international conflict, at least in many parts of the world, the security-industrial sector is booming. Indeed, whole branches of government, not just the police and the military, are devoting themselves to food security, energy security, data security, environmental security, and so on. The supply of threats seems disconnected from the demand for security. In people's daily lives, fear of crime, terrorism, and geopolitical chaos loom large. Nation-states, and local neighborhoods, invest in security, often in the same technology. There is no end in sight because the end appears as the means. The task of exploring security capitalism is made difficult by the number of domains touched by it and the myriad forms it takes, such as private policing, racialized urban planning, and mass surveillance.

Today there is much talk about surveillance capitalism, thanks to Shoshana Zuboff's analysis of Silicon Valley tech companies. But the focus on so-called surveillance capitalism obscures as much as it reveals. Meta, Alphabet, and Twitter, among others, have all been shown to be in cahoots with the US security state, to say nothing of China and Russia's digital platforms. And these relationships go back a long way.

In 1956, when Lockheed moved its missile systems center to Sunnyvale, California, there was little except fields in the area. Within a decade, Sunnyvale acquired thirty thousand new residents who spent their days developing microchips. Later, with Pentagon money and support, together with researchers from Stanford University, a battlefield communication system was developed in the Valley, the first "internet." Today, in the cafés of Sunnyvale, Mountain View, and Palo Alto, it is probable that the tech entrepreneur sitting at the next table has interacted with the security and defense sector.

Our use of *security capitalism* risks becoming a term that illuminates everything but spotlights nothing. Therefore, this book is composed of ethnographic essays. We will show that people are imprisoned by security capitalism, in their homes, neighborhoods, and worldviews. The bars are sometimes hard to see but the cage is real enough. The concept of security capitalism is not an effort to explain everything but, rather, a possible key for unlocking change.

Silver-haired and with a bookish air, Liam (pseudonym) could easily be mistaken for a lawyer or academic. People are often surprised to learn that he served for thirty years as a member of the Garda Síochána, the Irish police. As a young officer, he patrolled the villages and farmlands along the border that divides the Irish Republic from British-administered Northern Ireland.[1] The authorities on both sides dubbed the border region "bandit territory" during the Troubles, so named because covert military units, sectarian terrorists, and "ordinary decent criminals" infested the countryside and attempted to impose their law. In the United States, securitization flowers in the fissures created by race and class inequalities; in Ireland's border region, the fissures were also formed by centuries-old ethnic and religious conflict—to borrow from W. B. Yeats, "Great hatred, little room, . . . I carry from my mother's womb / A fanatic heart."[2]

The style of policing differed dramatically depending on what side of the border you were on. In British-administered Northern Ireland, the Royal Ulster Constabulary patrolled in armored cars, accompanied by paratroopers. South of the border, Liam and his colleagues patrolled unarmed and often on foot. And yet, they somehow kept the peace; they even solved a crime or two. Liam worked his way up from border patrol duties and, after ten years and much additional training, he was promoted to detective inspector and transferred to a large city, where he built cases against drug gangs. The last years of his policing career involved pioneering work on international criminal asset forfeiture. Following early retirement at age fifty-five, he opened a consultancy company specializing in organizational change. "Sure, I've been through so many organizations," he jokes. However, despite his considerable experience, he was shocked by the private security world. It took him a long time to appreciate the global scale, growing significance, and unrestrained ruthlessness of private security.

Today, policing faces a crisis of the imagination. Following decades of protests highlighting police violence, from the United States to the United Kingdom and South Africa to South America, calls for change are harder than ever to ignore. Reformers search for technical fixes for complex systemic problems; scholars search for progressive models that might be uprooted from their cultural context and successfully transplanted elsewhere;

abolitionists are trying to imagine a future with safety but without police.

While debates over the best course of action rage in academic and activist circles, policing is changing rapidly. Powerful corporate interests push for the unbundling of policing institutions to privatize services and strip assets. Because there is public support for law-and-order policies, police budgets remain high, and companies selling back-office services and crime-stopping solutions are returning handsome profits. For good or ill, modern policing happens in a maelstrom caused by competing forces. To navigate in a positive direction, we must understand where modern policing came from, the trends shaping it today, and the obvious barriers to meaningful change.

At first, Ireland may seem like a strange starting point. However, it is the country where modern policing was first tested. Liam's Garda Síochána undoubtedly has its share of scandals and controversies. Nevertheless, because Ireland is small and has only one law enforcement body, it offers an odd but helpful perspective on the challenges presented by providing security through policing. The ethnographic description of Liam's career foregrounds many of the most salient challenges. In each phase of his career, from the early years of street-level policing to international consulting, the principles that organize policing come to the fore. As we shall see, principles are important, but so also are practices, and when one considers principles and practices, one quickly realizes that policing must be reimagined from the foundations up.

For a long time, historians held that modern law enforcement began with Sir Robert Peel's Metropolitan Police, the unarmed "Bobbies" who patrolled the streets of nineteenth-century London. However, before Sir Robert tested modern policing on the English, so the saying goes, he tried it on the dog—the dog was Ireland.

In 1853, Frederick Engels wrote to Karl Marx about the situation in John Bull's other island,

> Ireland may be regarded as England's first colony and as one which, because of its proximity, is still governed exactly in the old way, and one can already notice here that the so-called liberty of English citizens is based on the oppression of the colonies. I have never seen so many gendarmes in any country . . . who are armed with carbines, bayonets, and handcuffs.[3]

Engels overstates his description of the Royal Irish Constabulary. These "gendarmes" were well-integrated into local communities, and Catholic sons of Ireland swelled their ranks. Moreover, at the time, there was more than one police force in the country (and, for that matter, dozens of police forces operated across Great Britain).[4] However, Engels's letter to Marx reads as prophecy by the end of the nineteenth century. Tenant farmers organized to agitate for land rights, and the Irish Constabulary found itself defending a doomed order. The

Constabulary's demise, and the fall of the British Empire in Ireland, was guaranteed when they yielded authority to the murderous Black and Tans, ex-military rabble shipped in to bolster British rule. Post-independence, these experiences informed the eventual decision to establish a civic guard operated by consent, trust, and moral authority rather than force of arms.

Irish history is illuminating, then, on several points. Firstly, history shows that a police force may be paramilitary and yet be accepted, or the opposite may hold, depending on the politics of the time. Secondly, politics is not external to policing. At protests today, one often hears the cry, "No justice, no peace!" However, the idea that justice is for all is relatively new. Policing protects the established societal order, using violence if deemed necessary and legitimate, against those who do not matter. When others—poor Irish farmers, racial minorities, migrants, and women, for example—demand their place in the polis, and insist that their lives matter, the order represented by the police must change or be changed. Thirdly, if there is sufficient will, the principles that organize policing may become a powerful lever with which to move the institution away from preservation of order for the few towards equality and justice for all.

When Liam first joined the Irish police, he knew he would spend much of his career working in and for local communities. Moreover, although there are a small number of armed units, most of his fellow officers wield only "their moral authority as servants of the people."[5] What if one must face down heavily armed individuals bent on resisting the rule of law? Lest we forget, Liam spent the first decade of his career patrolling the Northern Irish border, confronting members of a terrorist organization armed with assault rifles, anti-tank rocket launchers, and a vast quantity of plastic explosives. "We were never there for a shootout," Liam says. "We had a job to do, and in a weird way so did they. Respect given and received goes a long way even with their kind." Contrast this with the images of police terrorizing unarmed citizens circulated in the global media in recent years, and think also of the numerous cases of egregious police violence that resulted in no disciplinary action or acquittal at trial.

The legal principles that underpin policing deserve attention because of the violence they license and the institutional ethos they underwrite. Activists in the United States have long challenged the "qualified immunity" enjoyed by police officers in cases where deadly force is used against suspects. We must also attend to how the law licenses discretion and in so doing detaches police from the communities they ostensibly protect and serve. In *Castle Rock v. Gonzales 2005*, the US Supreme Court ruled that it is at an officer's "discretion" to involve herself in any number of matters, from domestic violence to mass shootings in schools. If the officer does involve herself, qualified immunity protects her against litigation for unlawful use of excessive force. In short, rather than serving the community at all costs, in the United States, police are encouraged to first protect themselves and use deadly force to do so.

Of course, principles only go so far. Practice must align with institutional values. During the time at the border, Liam claims he learned a profound lesson about what not to do. He was trusted to exchange intelligence with his Royal Ulster Constabulary counterparts because he looked bookish, "like a Protestant." He recalls accompanying Constabulary as they patrolled with British paratroopers in convoys of armored "Tangi" Land Rovers. Because urban streets in Ireland are narrow, and the patrols never knew when the next petrol bomb or sniper's bullet would come, they drove in low gear to enable rapid acceleration. Over time the gears frayed, and they began to screech their way through neighborhoods. South of the border, policing involved face-to-face negotiation; in the North, community policing was done by a "screaming porcupine" of armored trucks. The contrasting images stayed with Liam and, in the later consultancy phase of his career, became the basis of his PowerPoint presentations.

The Troubles ended with the Belfast Agreement in 1998. The Constabulary was rebranded as the Police Service of Northern Ireland (PSNI). The screeching Land Rovers were replaced or repaired and given a lick of new paint. Liam witnessed the dawn of this era. By the late 1990s, before he was reassigned, he saw the new PSNI officers, some unarmed, standing drinking cups of tea with neighborhood residents. The purpose, principles, oversight processes, and everyday practices had all shifted. Crime and terrorist activity declined precipitously. "Two jurisdictions," Liam says, "same approach, same result. It was like a natural experiment."

Liam recalls the early lessons he learned about policing with great sincerity, but he tends to edit out the subsequent years. After a decade spent in bandit territory, he was promoted and transferred to an urban anti-crime unit that aimed to disrupt drug gangs in disadvantaged neighborhoods. They found few glamorous kingpins, he admits, but plenty of poor children in search of money and status. The neighborhoods in his district were undergoing regeneration, property prices were skyrocketing, and a new shopping mall was under construction. The property developers and middle-class residents had no patience for his speeches about community policing. And so, time and again, Liam and his unit would follow an intelligence tip and speed into a neighborhood in a fleet of unmarked cars, only to find the chief suspect already left for school. Frustrations grew. They began to stop and frisk residents. Then, one day, they encountered a group of teenagers on a busy street, and when searched, some disclosed small quantities of marijuana. They radioed for a marked van but told the driver to take his time. They handcuffed the children wrist-to-ankle in a humiliating daisy chain. Passers-by watched and laughed. Liam caught the gaze of one child, and he realized that they had just turned a boy into a rage-filled criminal. "That's how you lose 'em."[6]

Liam became increasingly unhappy in his role as a gang-busting detective. At first, the job was exciting, but the stress on his body soon showed in regular injury and illness, and his mind searched for in vain meaning. Worse, the aggressive raids based on dubious intelligence yielded only community resentment. Rather than contemplate a different approach, the institutional response was to double down. Worse still, the entire model was, in Liam's view, calcifying a macho internal culture, which resisted oversight and was openly defiant of alternative approaches. Always the autodidact, and knowing that solutions had to be acceptable, he began to read and think about how criminal asset forfeiture might yield better results. He persuaded senior managers to establish a dedicated unit, swaying the conservative bureaucracy with the promise of revenue and media coverage. The unit took off, as did his career, and he found himself reporting to headquarters, collaborating with international policing bodies, and offering training to junior staff. His unit was soon staffed with well-trained civilians, as was a new crime analytics unit that management placed under his leadership. As one might expect, the expert layer of policing in and adjacent to central headquarters was staffed by personnel with little experience in street-level policing. Yet they were supremely comfortable turning loose information into actionable data and thus sending patrols screeching into disadvantaged neighborhoods. Policing, as Liam came to realize, was "out of whack," a phrase he picked up while training in the US, meaning that it was no longer vertically integrated but rather siloed, internally disconnected. Liam saw his next career move clearly: he decided to retire early and offer consultancy services to international policing bodies. He was experienced and well connected, and he foresaw the need for experts who might encourage positive change in organizations that could no longer understand themselves. He retired with a generous pension and traveled to Pakistan, Saudi Arabia, and Kenya before retreating into abstractions, disgusted by what he saw.

Liam's first significant consultancy role was a morally deflating experience. A United Nations project team commissioned him to bring European legal experts to Pakistan to review protocols for police interviews of suspects. Liam's local contact, a cheerful, chatty man, guided the delegation to the police station's basement where a dozen or so "suspects" were being tortured to "soften them up" before their formal, aboveground interview. Shocked, the UN delegation immediately retreated, first to their luxury hotel, then, realizing they were eyewitnesses, to the airport. Months later, Liam secured a new contract as a consultant in Saudi Arabia and Kenya. "The money was good, especially in the Middle East, but you had to leave your morals at the door," he confided. As he jetted around the world in search of more contracts, he became more aware of the sheer scale of the private security industry. Throughout his career, he focused on the modern institution of policing, so he paid little attention to the growth of its dark shadow, preferring to imagine private security as the domain of poorly paid "mall cops."

In his celebrated (as prophetic by security types) book *The Transformation of War,* Martin Van Creveld warned that we had entered an era in which traditional policing and military institutions are yielding to the booming security business. "The time may come when the organizations that comprise that business will, like the *condottieri* of old, take over the state."[7] Liam surveyed the world of security and arrived at the same conclusion. In Kenya and Saudi Arabia, private military contractors escorted him everywhere; the police he trained were either moonlighting as private guards or trying to insert themselves into the commercial security sector; when flying home, he recognized "the lads" selling scanners and processing systems to airports; arriving on Irish soil, he noted that there were more private security guards in his native land than national police. When Liam looked at the world, private security operators returned his gaze. What are the true dimensions of this business sector, and what is its precise impact on policing today?

Figures on security market size and growth are notoriously incomplete and generally do not count services delivered in partnership. However, what data there are suggest a striking pattern. Conservative estimates indicate that the commercial private security market is growing at 9 percent annually and is worth approximately $300 billion. In the United States, estimates suggest two million people are employed in the private security sector, meaning that private guards outnumber police by a ratio of 3:1. South Africa is home to one of the proportionally largest commercial security markets in the world. Private guards are often better armed, trained, and supported than their police counterparts. In one beach city frequented by the wealthy, the police station is equipped with a panic alarm that dials a private security company. Unsurprisingly, from South Africa to South Florida, private security operators are responsible for much violence. As we think back to the killing of unarmed Treyvon Martin in 2012 by a neighborhood watchman, the event that sparked the Black Lives Matter movement, we must be mindful that today fifteen US states have no requirement that armed security guards are trained. However, shocking though this is, one must look beyond street-level security to fully understand the growth of this sector.

In recent years, activists have called for the defunding of police, together with the unbundling of policing services. Even by just reflecting on Liam's policing career, we can easily see the very different dimensions of police activity, from patrolling to management and from forensic and analytics-based work to, essentially, the provision of social services. If nothing else, we must surely ask why do we send heavily armed police to intervene in domestic or mental health crises? But so-called unbundling, rather than being an obvious solution, reveals the already deep imbrication of modern policing with corporate interests. Organizations such as RAND and numerous neoliberal think tanks have promoted the unbundling of police services for over thirty years: they aim to privatize public services and release fixed asset value in the name of efficiency.[8] There is a logic to their proposal, but it is the cold management logic redolent of private consultancy that now dominates numerous public institutions. This relentless logic has already led to the privatization of many aspects of contemporary policing, swathes of the criminal justice process, and a significant portion of the prison system. As we have argued throughout this book, we are trapped by security, and there is no better illustration today than the line that stretches from the private security guard to the for-profit prison.

As Liam jetted about the world in search of consultancy contracts, the world of security seemed anything but flat. He was a creature spawned by a public security bureaucracy, but as time went on, he could no longer distinguish public from private and legitimate from illicit. Indeed, he gave up on claiming any real expertise. "I just sell stories, and common sense, for cash," he says.

Sometimes deep insights are expressed in common language. According to Liam, policing is "out of whack." The public desire for security is being answered by untrustworthy private operators, and traditional policing is simultaneously collapsing under the weight of external expectations and internal ineptitude. Despite this, police forces are either unwilling to make changes or are unable to contemplate change.

From Northern Ireland in the 1980s to North America today, the research literature is clear that the deployment of paramilitary force does not stop illicit activity but instead fosters community hostility. Despite this, from 1972 to 2018, paramilitary-style drug raids carried out by North American SWAT teams increased by 26,665 percent.[9] From poor Irish neighborhoods to Parisian banlieues, the research literature shows that stop-and-frisk policing is ultimately counterproductive, yet it continues, now bolstered by crime analytics software sold by private operators. Everywhere there are calls for more security, and private operators are answering those calls. We must surely conclude by asking: how might we reimagine policing for today's world such that it serves the modern polis?

We can certainly imagine divesting policing of its for-profit security elements, but should we be nostalgic for an earlier era when violent state-capitalism held a monopoly on the legitimate use of force. Moreover, we now have the means to identify and cast out racist, brutal, and ineffective elements within policing, but if we do so, we may be left with no apples, rotten or otherwise, in the barrel. The task of reimagining policing must begin with what ought to be, and not with efforts to tinker at the edges of the world that is.

There is yet another important lesson to be learned from Liam's career. He and his fellow Gardai patrolled Ireland's so-called bandit territory as community police. When facing heavily armed threats, they policed by consent, drawing on principles rather than violent practices. Strange though it may seem considering the risk involved, their de-escalatory approach was broadly effective, and was certainly the least-worst option available. However, years later, when he and his colleagues came roaring into poor urban neighborhoods in search of petty criminals, they also announced themselves as community police. A policy without principle is just an empty phrase. Liam, ever the careerist, did not challenge his superior officers on their abandonment of principle. Instead, he presented a palatable proposal to pursue criminal asset forfeiture. One might think of this episode as an illustration of "solutionism." In short, rather than grapple with the underlying cause of a societal problem, security is predisposed to seek palatable technical, scientific, or procedural solutions, ideally for a return, preferably a financial return.

Today, community policing is frequently touted as an example of international best practice—Liam never fails to push it as a universally applicable solution in his PowerPoint presentations. However, in Ireland and elsewhere, community policing is a contested term for a promiscuous set of law enforcement practices only loosely tied to the principle of policing by community consent.[10] For example, during the last decade, activists and political commentators have praised reformers in Newark, New Jersey, for their community-centered approach to public safety, which includes investment in an ecosystem of funded programs to reduce violence. However, New Jersey is also a frontrunner in the use of so-called risk terrain modeling, whereby crime hotspots are identified and hyper-policed by law enforcement and community workers.

What if we start to reimagine policing by beginning with principles rather than solutionism? From this perspective, would community policing look like an ideal-type solution or a least-worst approach? Interestingly, early discussion of community policing grappled with the principles at stake. Writing back in 1928, London Metropolitan Police Assistant Secretary H. Alker Tripp recognized that talk about his institution as a model for emulation was intellectually limiting and potentially dangerous. Tripp, a dyed-in-the-wool conservative, believed that policing should focus on preserving the "liberty" of his fellow countrymen, meaning that they should be free to enjoy their assets without interference. Alas, he says, "This nation of ours—as independent, high-spirited and freedom-loving a people as the world has ever seen—trussed itself up of its own free will, and handed over the whip to the police." He explains that this desire for security at the expense of liberty is the fault of new "publics" entering politics. Those people wish to be safe and secure, yet they demand "equality" simultaneously. Policing, he assured his readers, cannot square this circle—it presumes an unequal order of things. He concluded thus, "Some other policy, and some other agency perhaps, will then have to be invoked, after the failure of the police."[11]

Again, deep insights often come in simple language. H. Alker Tripp was a simple man. He understood that liberty, because it presumes inequality, must be enforced, ideally through the organized effort of the state. If all people are to be treated equally, security, in the sense of individuals seeking liberty separate from and armed against society, is society's fundamental challenge. In short, we can have equality and justice or the freedom to live behind walls protected from imagined monsters by real ones, but we cannot have both. We will continue to be trapped by security unless we plot our escape by starting with core principles.

CONCEPT NOTE: SOLUTIONISM

Around the world, from East Africa to North America, states and societies are constantly throwing simplistic technical "solutions" at complex social problems.[1] This disposition is especially pronounced when it comes to the provision of security. Although inequality predicts violent crime rates, the preference is always to switch on surveillance cameras rather than strive for equality. We know that a culture of impunity emboldens state violence, yet politicians and police chiefs prefer to invest in body-worn cameras rather than challenge systemic abuses of power. As Cedric Johnson argues, "technological fixes" are prevalent in policing precisely because they do not address deeper societal problems. Solutionism, then, generates profit for security capitalism while preserving the political status quo.[2]

As shown throughout this book, security capitalism flourishes in society's racial, class, and other fissures; it thrives wherever there is fear and anxiety. Security, in this sense, denotes infinitely regressive action rather than an objective to be reached, like safety or peace. Therefore, the so-called solutions pushed by security capitalism will either exacerbate existing problems or generate new ones. Companies sell phone-tracking services to parents anxious about their children's whereabouts. A few decades ago, using technology to track someone was just sinister. Today, however, gadgets are the thin end of the wedge. Parental anxiety has risen as threats to safety have fallen. Nonetheless, we see significant investment in AI software to monitor children's moods for indicators of potential self-harm or harm by others. A few decades ago, the idea that predictive software would guide police patrols was fantastical. However, security capitalism is already crossing the Rubicon: several law enforcement agencies are using predictive analytics to identify likely future offenders among schoolchildren.

Once security capitalism establishes a bridgehead, an endless line of gadgets, services, ways of working, and expert ways of thinking inevitably follow. Of course, solutions often exist before there is a marketplace for them; and a market, as already explained, may be created wherever there is a societal fissure, weakened public institution, or pervasive fear. Once security capitalism creates a problem and sells a solution, people are encouraged to believe in this good work and do more of it. After all, who does not wish safety for their children? Every solution, then, is coded with ideology. Like gated residences, violent policing, and homeland security, the entire security edifice relies on public support, consent, and cooperation.

A massive industry is producing security solutions with the willing cooperation of applied academics and reformist activists. Some academics and reformers are doubtless in it for cash or status. However, many are sincere in believing that whatever the problem is, the answer will inevitably involve technology and technocratic policy. This is what we mean when we speak of solutionism. Historian of science Evgeny Morozov popularized the term when describing how digital designers theorize rather than investigate problems and provide answers before asking even basic questions. He worries that important societal questions are increasingly being outsourced to designers and other experts who promptly bury them in the technological infrastructure of our solutionist society.

There is hope, as Morozov sees it, right in front of us, in our classrooms. Evidence shows that designers given additional training in subjects like ecology, psychology, and anthropology tend to develop more innovative and sustainable products and services than those with only a systems-based education.[3] What if we take this insight and apply it to security? Too often, corporations release security technology with only the briefest wave to "ethics" or responsible innovation. It may be possible to solve the problem of solutionism and thereby challenge contemporary securitization by educating a new generation to ask meaningful questions rather than seek profit with ineffective solutions.

Mark first met Steve (pseudonym), an airport police inspector, at an invitation-only workshop in 2015. The workshop, sponsored by IBM, was about recruiting new technology and design for the fight against terrorism. The delegates included academics, industry representatives, and security experts from Europe and North America. The industry representatives showcased futuristic surveillance systems, while the security consultants, mainly retired senior police officers, described past terrorist attacks and future threat scenarios. The public's experience of security was not discussed. Instead, delegates focused on available pots of EU research and development funding. The machinery of security capitalism hummed in the conference room.

At six-foot-four and wearing a police uniform, Steve stood out among the workshop delegates. He had recently been promoted to police training manager for a major British airport and was genuinely excited to make external contacts and learn about transformative technologies. Security bureaucracies are notoriously hierarchical and involuted. Steve dreamed of one day establishing an international training center. He would need to slowly, patiently cultivate the support of his superiors. In the interval, he aimed to become, as he put it, "the man in the know." However, it soon became apparent that his interests differed from the other delegates. "I think they're on a different planet," he confided to Mark. As each PowerPoint slideshow faded into the next, he strategically repositioned himself closer to the exit door.

Halfway through the workshop agenda, a design industry CEO presented a series of futuristic counter-terror "solutions" for airports, most notably ambient environments, denoting moveable walls and barriers that adjust autonomously in response to algorithmic crowd flow analysis. The CEO presented a lengthy analysis of the 2007 terror attack on Glasgow Airport to ground the benefits of his designs. The presentation animated the audience, and a wave of suggestions for investments in surveillance technology came from the floor. Steve was intimately familiar with the Glasgow incident for various reasons. Indeed, he experienced a similar but failed attack at his airport. He believed he was an expert but was soon to discover that he was just a "practitioner" or "end-user" in the eyes of the other delegates.

To his credit, the designer acknowledged that the Glasgow attack was a curious one. Two medical professionals, Bilal Abdullah and Kafeel Ahmed, worked in the city's main hospital but led secret lives as part of a Jihadist network. The network planned a bomb attack on a well-known LGBTQ+ nightclub in London, but their explosive device failed to detonate. The intelligence services used a mobile phone accidentally left at the scene to identify the network members. Spooked, Abdullah and Ahmed decided to crash a Jeep packed with gas canisters, fuel, and nails into Glasgow's airport terminal. However, the Jeep became impaled on a door bar. Ahmed exited the vehicle, drenched himself in petrol, and set himself ablaze. Abdullah threw Molotov cocktails at the terminal. According to the tabloid media, kicks and punches from Glaswegian taxi drivers and airport workers overpowered the terrorists. According to the police, one of their officers, unarmed and off duty, took control of the situation.

At the IBM workshop, the designer summarized the incident for conference delegates before assuring them that his smart cameras and automatic bollards would have prevented the terrorists from ever reaching the terminal. At this point, Steve lost his composure. Exasperated, he interjected, pointing out that the Glasgow terrorists were under active MI5 surveillance, yet they still carried out the attack. He described how the airport's experienced CCTV controller noticed no erratic driving and initially recorded a traffic incident rather than a terror attack. Moreover, long after order was restored, armed police arrived, followed by black-clad Special Forces, and, finally, members of the secret intelligence service announced themselves. The three branches of state power proceeded to shout at one another over who had jurisdiction. Steve concluded, "Glasgow, Belfast, London . . . airports everywhere are policed by the likes of me. We meet, talk, share, you know, work together to keep people safe and prevent unlawful interference with civil aviation. None of this [he gestured towards the presenter's PowerPoint slideshow] is of any help to me." After a brief pause and not even a hint of embarrassment, the workshop participants continued to discuss potential investments. Steve's mistake was to conflate everyday safety with industrial-strength security. The workshop participants were members of security capitalism's cognitive elite. They knew little and cared even less about his operational world; they were only interested in generic problems and scalable security solutions. Though he did not know it at the time, Steve made a career choice between his (perhaps antiquated) values and joining the carnival of security capitalism. He decided to remain true to his values, a fatal career choice.

Following the workshop, Mark stayed in regular contact with Steve. A year later, they collaborated on a six-month ethnographic study of airport policing.[1] Mark followed the shift routine in Steve's airport as he and his colleagues directed traffic, sought help for mentally unwell passengers, intervened in drunken brawls, and completed reams of paperwork. He listened as they recalled extraordinary moments, such as an unexpected childbirth or the day one of their officers foiled a Provisional IRA bomb attack. They emphasized constant engagement with the community, denoting passengers, airline staff, drivers, cleaners, and thousands of other workers—it was a tip-off from a cleaner that led to the interdiction of the IRA bombers. However, as they saw it, accidents and violent incidents happen no matter what one does: security is never perfect, and it never ends.

Scale is the most palpable security challenge facing the modern airport. There were approximately seven billion airline passenger trips in 2022—the number of trips per annum continues to rise—many of which took place on the massive grounds of an international airport. One police officer described the impossibility of the task that he faces thus,

> We would preach a community-based policing approach here, but whilst it's the correct approach, I think, for what we do, but community to my mind, the traditional community, if you like, is relatively static. ... We've had between 25 and 28 million passengers . . . if you're defining community, they are not part of your community, but they are part of who we deal with. [. . .] The role of the police officer is to make sure that can they get into the airport. Do they know where they are going? Are they safe while they are in the airport? Do they have a feeling of safety? Do they know who to contact if there's a problem? You know you will see lots of the incidents. You can get the stats you know: six, seven thousand incidents we go through in the year.

Two thousand of them could be medical incidents. ... We want to be the community police, like you would have in a village. (interview 2016)

Many contemporary jobs involve Sisyphean effort. Surgeons will try to save each patient knowing they cannot prevent every death. Contemporary societies, because of their scale, place trust in professional expertise and the professional work ethic. However, though hardworking, Steve and his police and security colleagues are not wholly trustworthy. Over six months of ethnographic "shadowing," Mark noted their ethnic, gender, and class biases. He pointed out that there was no legislative basis for their self-anointed role as community protectors, and he recommended reflection on professional ethics and training on the fundamentals of human rights. That said, their vision, which emphasizes public safety through community engagement, is a welcome heresy in the faith-based world of militarized airport security.

Multiple case examples show that when a disaster happens, it is the likes of Steve, his colleagues, and their wider community who save lives and restore order. They represent a flawed security model, and yet they offer much more than the expensive theories and experimental gadgets of security capitalism. Airports have long been laboratories where security technology is developed and deployed. Today, airports are also living laboratories where societal values are tested.

The airport is an architectural reflection of the modernist dream of individual freedom and adventure without risk, without the chaos that comes with true freedom. Steve's home airport is illustrative. The military constructed it during the 1940s, but upper-middle-class travelers soon arrived and quickly overran the place. Conscious that the wealthy are risk adverse, a private company built an impersonal modernist terminal in the 1950s that gave splendid views of airplanes taking off and landing safely—at the time, it was common to construct airports that looked like serene train stations to soothe the jittery nerves of first-time flyers. The 1960s brought cheaper flights, crowds, and shopping opportunities. The 1970s brought terrorists. During those decades, hijackings were disturbingly frequent, with estimates suggesting an average of two incidents per month in the United States. And yet, security did not become the obsession that it is today. This began to change in 1972 when three men boarded Southern Airways Flight 49, departing Birmingham, Alabama and hijacked the airliner following a refueling stop. They demanded an end to police brutality in Black communities, $10 million, and a conversation with President Richard Nixon. The hijackers became frustrated by the slow response by the authorities and insisted that Flight 49 circle the Oakridge nuclear facility. The incident ended many hours later in Havana, Cuba. However, the threat to a nuclear laboratory changed the world.[2] Slowly at first, around the world, including in Steve's airport, the modern terminal became a place for shopping, dining, dreams of adventure, and crushing boredom, all wrapped in a security blanket.

Airport police sometimes refer to the air-side zone (after security screening) as the "sterile" or "clean" space. Identity documents, surveillance technologies, and armed police keep the clean space separated from the dangerous and chaotic outside. In the wake of September 11, 2001, airports invested heavily in physical and software designs to fortify themselves against future attacks. Steve and his older colleagues remember their terminals before the armed patrols, blast-proof structures, and ubiquitous surveillance cameras. They do not believe people are safer today because of the sterility enforced by security measures. That said, since 9/11, there have been no terrorist acts recorded in the airport's incident log. However, members of the public are deathly afraid of terrorism—it regularly features as a leading fear in public surveys, and a recent YouGov poll showed that 80 percent of Americans approve of anti-terrorism measures. Politicians, policymakers, and senior police are all willing to stoke fears. Politicians and policymakers share a nervous system with public sentiment. As for the senior managers, to quote Steve, "They don't want to be caught with their trousers down" should a disaster happen. And so, the carnival of security capitalism, showcasing the latest snake-oil-based solution, is welcomed into public institutions. Senior managers permit surveillance software testing and host the latest workshop on violent "radicalization." They will be rewarded if they introduce a security innovation, especially a cost-saving one. No matter how efficacious it is, investment in a gadget will protect the careerist from criticism should things go wrong. Moreover, such an investment connects the careerist to major corporations and, thus, to the lucrative world of postretirement consulting. And so, to quote Steve, "They drink the Kool-Aid."

In 2016, while Mark was working with Steve to carry out an ethnographic evaluation of airport policing, senior airport managers asked for their attendance at a meeting to decide on procuring full-body scanners, which at the time used backscatter x-ray technology. The discussion did not focus on efficacy or ethics. Instead, senior managers were envious of a rival airport that had already installed body scanners. Therefore, they were delighted that a former colleague, now working for the multinational supplier, had promised them a free trial and possibly a purchase discount. Public acceptance of the intrusive technology was dismissed confidently by a senior manager: "It's futuristic security. The public will think it's cool!" Steve just shrugged. "Sure," he said, "They probably will."

If the public willingly accepts intrusive security technology, and if people are prepared to sacrifice freedom to feel safe, then it is no easy task to point to a gilded cage and call it a prison. The task of countering counterterrorism must involve demonstrating that anti-terror measures are not just harmless inconveniences and that we have been sold these measures based on lies. Survey after survey of public sentiment shows that people believe the threat of terrorism is real and that security technologies are a proportionate response. Nobody wants to be trapped in an airport terminal with armed psychopaths after all. But security experts have a limited, qualified interest in preserving life.

In 2016, terrorists attacked Brussels Airport. Before the smoke cleared, international experts recommended installing internal blast-proof doors that could be closed in the event of an attack, sealing off sections of the terminal and thereby slowing the attack by sacrificing a few innocent civilians. Mid-ranking police and security officers working in European aviation voiced their objections, technical and moral, often in colorful language. Here we have the security-industrial complex giving serious consideration to locking civilians in a security trap with their attackers. This proposal, and others like it, show that security capitalism produces remedies worse than the illness to which they are applied—in ancient Greek, this is pharmakon, a poisonous cure.

During the past two decades, airports have seen investments in inappropriately intrusive and shamelessly discriminatory technology, together with unnecessary precautionary procedures, from subjecting toddlers to pat-downs to scanning people for microfacial expressions of deceit. Of course, we must spotlight such egregious examples to undermine the legitimacy of security capitalism. However, we must also attend to the wellsprings of counterterrorism's legitimacy and public acceptance of and trust in security, namely the "scientific" security knowledge used to reassure the public that intrusive and discriminatory measures are necessary.

Much of an airport's security infrastructure is invisible to the public, and the lack of visibility gives the strange rules and beeping machines a mystifying authority. However, the sharp end of security is visible to passengers: uniformed guards, guns, cameras, scanners, and other gadgets. The infrastructure and the visible superstructure emerge from a knowable production process. In universities and global corporations, engineers, philosophers, computer scientists, and sociologists work for the security-industrial complex. They are experts in solutionism, the evacuation of complexity from sociality to enable techno-scientific intervention in a predefined problem. The problem may be invented or intractable (take "radicalization," for example), and the solution may be expensive and ineffective (take mass surveillance, for example), but such problems are just fuel for solutionism.

During the past two decades, academics, public intellectuals, and intelligence agents have promoted the idea that a terrorist attack is just the final stage of a process that is knowable by experts. The process begins with radicalization. Radicals choose a target and probe it for weakness, then strike, leaving society to deal with the fallout. Each stage has a body of expertise devoted to it, each with an impressive-sounding name—counter-radicalization, surveillance and analysis, anticipatory security, and emergency response management. These are the pillars of counterterrorism. Security capitalism loves these pillars because they simplify the complex and unmanageable reality. A simplified reality is, after all, open to solutionism. Terrorists may target an airport, and we should anticipate this somehow. The terrorists will probably behave abnormally. Intelligent cameras may detect the erratic driving of panicky terrorists. Therefore, we should invest in artificial intelligence for surveillance. The logic here is specious, and the solutions rest on nothing but pseudo-scientific sand.

The word *radicalization* is meaningless. It might refer to a violent extremist or angry artist.[3] Despite this terminological inexactitude, governments pour billions of dollars into the search for a typical radicalization pathway. (One scholar recently set out the potential variables on a colorful "radicalization pyramid"). These specious theories persuaded Hizb ut-Tahrir al-Islami (the Party of Liberation) to target young people using the latest academic model—citing poor results, they later reverted to recruitment by family and friends.

It was direct exposure to world events, together with the influence of family and friends, that led the two medics to attack Glasgow Airport in 2007. One year after the Glasgow attack, MI5, the British domestic intelligence service, leaked a classified report on radicalization to the press. The report, which reviewed hundreds of terror incidents, showed that terrorists are unremarkable *men*, reasonably well-educated and culturally integrated individuals who are not particularly religious.[4] There is no typical pathway to violent extremism.

Of course, one might object here. Governments spend billions on countering radicalization each year; academic centers devote themselves to studying this problem. There must be some foundation beneath this massive structure. A decade ago, the leading scholar of radicalization, Peter Neumann examined the quality of research in the area and concluded that over one-third of scholarship failed to meet basic methodological standards.[5] Indeed, a recent review of the UK's counterterrorism Prevent program showed that it was peculiarly poor at detecting potential terrorists but rather good at placing innocent people under surveillance. Educators, local leaders, and healthcare workers, especially those from Muslim communities, were encouraged to refer children to counterterrorism officials if their "style of dress" changed or they became "angry and disrespectful." Accordingly, counterterrorism officials could not spot the few would-be terrorists among the many reports of troubled teens and Marxist students. With all these deep flaws, how is it possible for counter-radicalization programs to continue? The answer to this question is available in a government review. The Independent Review of Prevent tells us that, despite the questionable efficacy, counterterrorism is a fundamentally political project. "A period of intensive and particularly devastating attacks" could, the report tells us repeatedly, "erode confidence" in the ability of government to protect their citizens from terrorism.[6] In politics, no confidence means no job.

The counter-radicalization pillar is undoubtedly without a solid foundation, but what of the other pillars? Surely the intelligence community can detect and intercept would-be terrorists. However, when one examines attacks, one often finds that the terrorists were under surveillance while they executed their plans. Those plots that are "foiled" often turn out to be failures on the part of the terrorists rather than successes on the part of the authorities.[7] Terrorism is stressful after all. Targets must be scouted, and mistakes are made. Hence the third and fourth pillars of counterterrorism are anticipatory security measures, such as the use of identification technology and on-site screening, and emergency management.

Especially since September 11, 2001, airports have seen a massive increase in the use of surveillance and identification technology. Technologies are increasingly interoperable, and they leak into the commercial realm. In the departure hall, your face is matched to your documents, whereas in a duty-free store, the same technology tracks your gaze and informs store managers about how best to adjust product placement. Because these technologies are designed to match bodies to data-rich documents, it is still unclear how effective they are at preventing an attack by an unknown terrorist with "clean skin." Therefore, digital surveillance is augmented by behavioral detection systems. The US Department of Homeland Security runs a $1 billion per annum program called Screening Passengers by Observational Technique (SPOT), which trains staff to look for abnormal signs of fear, stress, or deception in crowds. The Government Accountability Office reviewed the system in 2013 and found that it offered results that were the same or only slightly better than chance.

The average British airport may have several law enforcement agencies present, from transport police to specialist counterterror police, and each may have behavioral detection officers trained to different standards. Mark participated in the training of behavioral detection officers in several European airports and noted that many of their secretive techniques involved little more than creating a minor disruption or talking points for waiting crowds, such as the arrival of a K9 unit, and then chatting to passengers, questioning those who stood out in reaction to the disruption. Confessions of malfeasance often took the form of passengers being surprised by the sight of uniformed police, then confiding to an undercover officer that they were smuggling contraband such as marijuana.

Steve trains police on behavioral detection. He is clear that, beneath everything, the goal is to get officers to know airport workers while on patrol. Cleaners, servers, porters are "a thousand eyes and ears" to quote Steve, "they will tell you if there's something suspicious, and if there is, just walk up to the person and talk to them.

There's usually a good explanation. And if there is an emergency, these people are your friends . . . and deputies." Thus, beneath the billion-dollar investments in biometrics, behavioral detection, and emergency response we see the layer of public safety-oriented activity dismissed by security capitalists as the "practitioner" knowledge of mere "end users."

Today, there is a tremendous political and public desire to live in a state of risk-free security. Terrorism is mercifully rare these days. It is declining even in the world's conflict zones. However, deadly incidents have a disproportionate impact on the public imagination. Terrorists know this, and so they blow things out of proportion. They choose targets—public gatherings, symbolic spaces, airports—that will shock and intimidate. If a state fails in its duty to protect the public, confidence will be lost, and heads will roll. If the state does its job well, bad things will not happen. If nothing bad happens, then a risk-free world becomes the expectation. It is an obscene fact of our age that as tolerance of risk declines, the demand for security grows. By manipulating risk and fear, security capitalism ensnares societies while producing the conditions for its profitability.

The safety offered by traditional police and security types is uneven, incomplete, and ethically problematic.[8] Security capitalism promises a safe world where futuristic gadgets and impressive-sounding methodologies will detect evildoers, perhaps even before they choose the wrong path. But behind the academic language and technical wizardry, we find an alliance of public sector careerists and commercial interests. Their priority is not public safety, and when push comes to shove, they and we are reliant on a traditional if problematic workforce. It is important to tell this story to the public, and to take every opportunity to point out the anti-social dimensions of counterterrorism. We must challenge the claims to efficacy; de-catastrophize risk. We must also attack its soft underbelly. Contemporary counterterrorism is only possible because of public acceptance, and acceptance is, more than efficacy, a source of legitimacy. Right now, university campuses house centers for the study of "radicalization," intelligence studies, and homeland security "fusion centers," and the myriad other pseudo-intellectual activities required to sustain counterterrorist myths. We can counter counterterrorism at home by countering the myths that sustain it.

Steve no longer works in airport policing. Global travel shrank dramatically during the COVID-19 pandemic, and once bustling airports resembled abandoned malls. Initially, he volunteered to do extra shifts to help operate a transit medical center. However, the lack of proper staff screening bothered him, and he determined to find a new career outside of security bureaucracies. He is now a student of human rights law.

CONCEPT NOTE: SECURITY-INDUSTRIAL COMPLEX

Before World War II, America's arms industry represented a modest 1 percent of its GDP, but that figure had risen to a staggering 40 percent by the 1960s. In his 1961 farewell address to the nation, US President Dwight D. Eisenhower warned that a giant "military-industrial complex" had wrapped its coils around democratic institutions. Antiwar activists adopted Eisenhower's phrase as their own. However, the thirty-fourth president was no peacenik: he wished to strike a balance between the state's duty to provide security and the noble desire for "perpetual peace."

Eisenhower could not have predicted the collapse of Communism, the end of the Cold War, or the subsequent unification of Europe. He would undoubtedly have been surprised to learn that in 2023 American expenditure on all aspects of security and defense is likely to top $1.4 trillion for the first time. Moreover, he would have found it incomprehensible that Europe's combined defense spending is now over $300 billion annually. Countries such as France, Italy, and even peace-loving Sweden have long supported large but discreet arms companies—Germany's Heckler & Koch is famous for making guns, while Volkswagen and BMW are better known for their cars.

Europe now describes itself as the Security Union in official documents. Contrary to popular belief, security and defense are not separate sectors, with one focused on international relations and the other on the homeland. Europe, like America, has a sprawling yet coherent security-industrial complex. The European security-industrial complex escapes public attention because of its jigsaw structure, with each nation-state's sector being a component piece. Patience is required to piece together the whole picture. Public attention is also distracted by Europe's saintly self-image, blurred further by the language of Brussels policymakers. For years, the EU has sent weapons to dubious foreign governments through the European Peace Facility. It is all very profitable, and Orwellian too. Following the 2022 Russian invasion of Ukraine, EU governments issued the Versailles Declaration, which promised a golden age for the sector that has already given us Leopard tanks and Panzerfaüst rockets.

But one might reasonably object here: isn't the phrase "military-industrial complex" sufficient, pointing as it does to the centrality of the defense sector? No, even before the end of the Cold War, the US defense sector repositioned itself in the broader field of security.[1] "Were the Soviet Union to sink tomorrow under the waters of the ocean," diplomat and historian George Kennan explained, "the American military-industrial complex would have to remain, substantially unchanged, until some other adversary could be invented."[2] The end of the Cold War brought corporate consolidation in the security sector but no peace dividend, and the events of September 11, 2001, brought forever wars against real and imagined adversaries.

Today, the security-industrial sector is multipolar. China, India, Israel, and others have powerful defense and security sectors. Russia has its "metal eaters," a single state-controlled arms exporter, and an official military that operates hand-in-glove with Wagner mercenaries. We focus on Europe and North America in this book because the EU and US represent over 70 percent of global arms production. Moreover, this is where the future of security is packaged and sold. Scholars and activists have already used the phrase "security-industrial complex" to describe the rise of mass digital surveillance and the privatization of policing. In this book, we explore counterterrorism in airports and the rise of European homeland security. These domains are clearly part of a security-industrial complex that is expanding and growing ever more dangerous.

In the United States, traditional national security, defense, and policing agencies are coming together on university campuses as think tanks and data "fusion centers." They claim to be battling foreign and domestic threats. In truth, the security-industrial complex decides what counts as a threat and what does not. Russian hackers and environmental activists are today's threats; tomorrow, it could be you!

5 RECLAIM HOMELAND SECURITY

In 2012, the European Union received the Nobel Peace Prize for advancing peace and human rights. That same year, Mark was invited to a European Commission workshop on counterterrorism hosted by Sarah (pseudonym), an influential security consultant. Although the workshop roster included senior EU officials and even a head of state, Sarah was the real star of the show. Designer sunglasses pushing back her mane of red hair, she progressed through the opening reception, stopping to greet business contacts as if they were close friends. At one point, she barged into a clique of corporate representatives and confided, "Henri is retiring this year!" She nodded in the direction of a nondescript French official before leaning in with, "I need another Henri, and rapidly!" One suspects that the executives took the instruction. That year, Sarah's firm raked in over €1 million in direct funding from the European Commission, and significant funds also flowed from consultancy and "training" contracts with French companies.

Sarah, a former multinational executive, struck out on her own during the late 1990s. She opened a small consultancy specializing in US-EU commercial cooperation. Then on September 11, 2001, terrorists struck at the beating heart of the global economy. Suddenly everything was a matter of security. Like Emperor Caligula, Sarah was reborn overnight, emerging as a "security expert." She quickly established a reputation for bringing different national and institutional stakeholders together to bid for European funding. Her early projects were, she confesses, just networking opportunities in disguise. Nevertheless, by adopting what the philosopher Elisabeth Lasch-Quinn calls a "posture of knowingness," she was soon shaping the sector in which she operated:

> When I went into security first, having come from industry, I understood the industrial environment well, that industry responds to demand, or tries to create demand among end-users, and how it tries to pull in the bits of professions or academia that suits them. Take Microsoft, IBM, and the like, they create the demand to suit what they have already developed—that's their raison d'être. . . .
> I looked at how security research in the European Union was developing, and what happened was **preparatory work**, based on the **Group of Personalities**.
> This was all post 9/11 of course, and you could see that everyone had their own desires. . . . They were never

thinking about the big-picture future, just their own short-term future. And academics were the same; and industrialists were the same with their quarterly returns, profit, and shareholder value. It became obvious that a bridge was needed. . . . But you couldn't put institutions together; you had to pick individuals and work with them (interview 2020 [our emphasis]).

Sarah's comments on the production of demand, and the importance of lateral networks, are striking, but who or what is the Group of Personalities, and what exactly is preparatory work?

In the wake of 9/11, and the subsequent invasion of Afghanistan, the EU gathered the so-called Group of Personalities to guide the future direction of European security.[1] The Personalities included EU officials, representatives of arms companies, and giant information technology corporations. They held that European industry was losing ground to its North American counterpart, especially when it came to public investment in security research. The Personalities felt that a figure of around €1 billion would be sufficient starting capital for a large-scale research and development initiative. "It was a shot in the arm," according to Sarah. The money arrived, and preparatory work began on the European Security Research Program. The Personalities immediately populated an oversight board with their nominees. Furthermore, by supervising the disbursement of public funds to themselves, the Personalities answered the ancient Roman poet Juvenal's famous question, "Quis custodiet ipsos custodes?" (Who will watch the watchers?)]

One of the more revealing statements issued by the Personalities is their Research for a Secure Europe report, which demands public research funding to support the full "exploitation" of scientific, technological, and industrial strength. The report reveals bold plans to merge defense with homeland security, but it also reveals a desire to somehow maintain the language of peace and justice while growing profits in security-capitalist enterprises. According to the report, an effective security program,

> should maximize the benefits of multi-purpose aspects of technologies. . . . It should look at the "crossroads" between civil and defense applications and foster cross-sector transformation and integration of technologies. . . . It would foster cross-border cooperation, increase European industrial competitiveness, and strengthen Europe's research base. . . . Europe's vision of security must therefore embrace a notion of "Internal Security" that can include a genuine feeling of well-being and safety for its citizens, while respecting its values of human rights, democracy, rule of law and fundamental freedoms.[2]

Here, security, and military defense, are governed as matters of industrial capitalism, and the report deflects concerns about the manufacture of weapons of war with pious incantations. In Brussels, to paraphrase George Orwell, words fall on facts like soft snow, burying the truth under layers of hypocrisy.

Like many consultants at the time, Sarah scanned the Research for a Secure Europe report looking for opportunities, as if it were an invitation to tender for work. To secure massive research and development contracts for cooperation and technology adoption, security corporations needed to involve public bodies as "end-users," and bring them together with experts in matters such as ethics and the societal impact of technology. Sarah immediately understood the opportunity presented in the report. Her company would be the bridge that linked end-users with powerful international corporations and applied academics. Her company would contribute to multimillion-euro contracts by offering a critical analysis of securitization—an analysis that would not be too critical, of course. As she saw it, the key was to offer standardized methods for ensuring that projects were compliant with human rights and legal norms around, say, privacy. With sufficient "safeguards" in place, legitimate criticism could be encompassed, and projects that used vast public resources to push surveillance technology into society could proceed.

On top of this, the growing security market involved more than immediate institutional or organizational needs. Security capitalism was poised to chase profit into the mysterious but threatening future, an endless and easily manipulated market. The threat of terrorism may be moderate or low in any given commercial airport, and the efficacy of smart CCTV, for example, may be unproven. However, the canny consultant could use scenarios, foresight exercises, or one's jealousy of a competitor airport to push "future needs." During those early years, it was critically important to understand, as Sarah did, that actual security, that is, public safety, was not the primary goal of security research and development. Instead, the goal was to stimulate the European security-industrial sector.

Supported by industry lobbyists, in 2010, Sarah was nominated as an evaluator for large-scale funding proposals within the Research Program. When she looked around Brussels conference rooms where billions of euros were disbursed, she saw so-called experts with outdated skills stuck in bureaucratic silos. These men—and they were mostly men—would never appreciate the picture painted by the Personalities. They reduced society to areas of concern, from airports to cities, each with specific matters of concern, from terrorism to hacking, matters that were to be responded to with technology, from military force to futuristic "smart dust." The picture is always changing because the future is constantly generating new concerns. As Sarah put it, "All I had to do was color between the lines."

What did these projects consist of exactly? A disinterested reader, after all, may consider security as a vital matter and hold that cross-border EU governance may have positive benefits, and perhaps even the Research for a Secure Europe report is correct to propose that Europe is "vulnerable" to "underwater threats." Perhaps not. Logic may also become trapped by security. Many people reason that without security and defense spending "we" cannot protect our values, freedom, and way of life from our enemies. But the point, of course, is to insist on a clear articulation of what's at stake. Not all threats are real, nor are all problems solvable with technical solutions; perhaps there are cases where it would be better to invest in accountable community safety rather than dehumanizing surveillance. After all, it is public money. From 2010 onwards, Sarah could see how the public's money was being spent.

Over a decade, Sarah became an influential player in the EU's security sector. She fully inhabited the role of security expert, frequently appearing in the news media and authoring think pieces for popular publications. Research institutes and government offices would ask her to join their funding bids to add the weight that her name carried. The projects were of varying quality. She described the whole enterprise as Willy Wonka's Chocolate Factory: the products were sometimes silly and frequently downright sinister. During bacchanalian project dinners with her consortium members, Sarah could be relied upon to tell stories about strange R&D projects that "should never have seen the light of day." Her audience always appreciated her description of the "lonely Finnish robot" (her title), an autonomous vehicle designed to patrol Finland's frozen border with Russia noiselessly so as not to frighten the wildlife. Her punch line played on the term "mission creep." However, on occasion, she would inform her lis-

teners that she reviewed the robotic system on behalf of
the European Commission at a fair organized by weapons
manufacturers. Strangely, perhaps blinded by the European Union's saintly self-image or comforted by the inef-
fectual work of Finnish roboticists, Sarah and her
colleagues seemed able to erect a mental wall between
their enterprise and the adjacent business of war. For a
long time now, British, French, and Italian companies
have jockeyed with each other at trade fairs to sell jet
fighters and laser-guided missile systems to Saudi Arabia,
and the Saudi Kingdom used those weapons to turn
Yemen's children into charcoal.

The distant rumble of war did not keep Sarah, or her
collaborators, awake at night, yet she was existentially
troubled by one of the projects she was asked to assess by
the Commission. In 2009, the EU granted €11 million to
INDECT (Information Systems Supporting Observa-
tion, Searching, and Detection for Security of Citizens in
Urban Environment). The project was led by Polish academics and police, and it included a strong EU-wide network of universities and law enforcement agencies. Like
many of the EU homeland security projects from this
era, it promised to solve complex societal problems—in
this case, terrorism, human trafficking, and child por-
nography—by opening private and sensitive public data
to algorithmic searches.

The major challenge of large-scale multinational projects
is the management of individual contributions and simul-
taneous maintenance of overall cohesion. A successful

project is always one that keeps to the agreed plan of work. However, INDECT suffered from mission creep. Researchers decided to also examine violence at sporting events. Therefore, video surveillance became an important project tool, and suddenly drones were needed. The researchers reasoned that any threat could be predicted if one had sufficient data. Therefore, the project team sought to include more and more data and analyze it using algorithmic surveillance systems. Overwhelmed by their engineering brilliance, the project team made a video to explain their work to the European Parliament. Superficially rational, silly, yet sinister, the short video depicts a "terrorist" being identified by INDECT surveillance cameras when stealing secret material. A high-speed car chase with police ensues, and the terrorist is apprehended by heavily armed black-clad men before being driven away in an unmarked van.[3]

One assumes that the promotional video's intended message was that national security demanded the latest integrated surveillance system. The message the public received was that the European Union was about to switch on an electronic panopticon, starting in Poland. The online hacker community Anonymous weighed in decrying the "undemocratic features in the EU which mostly hide under the cloak of suppression of terrorism." The European Commission responded with their own video, which claimed that the public's fears were unjustified—INDECT was merely a research project, a spokesman explained reassuringly, and there was an official mechanism for making complaints.[4]

Behind the scenes, Sarah explained, the Commission was wounded, and the drive towards common defense and homeland security was suddenly on shaky ground. The EU's self-image was of a Nobel Peace Prize winner after all, a champion of democracy and human rights. The public should trust the EU even though it was building a vast security sector because surveillance and black-clad commandos would only ever be used against bad people, such as traffickers or terrorists. The EU understood itself to be essentially benign. INDECT, Sarah explained, was more than a single rogue project that colored outside the lines. It revealed a grotesque truth about European security: the Polish project leaders did not misinterpret the brief; rather, they fulfilled their funding mandate a little too precisely and without dressing it up as a benign research program. It was a mass surveillance project paid for by a publicly funded security-industrial complex. The scales fell from Sarah's eyes. She crossed the aisle to sit with the activists at EU security workshops and events. However, she still needed to earn a living.

Sarah's pivot to a more critical stance on security was slow and lucrative. She realized that security systems, and especially the technologies that interface with the public, were often ignorant of human variation, along the lines of gender and race, for example, and were equally ignorant of cultural variation, such as responses to authority. Likely because of her impressive résumé and massive network of contacts, she drove early projects on matters such as bias, gendered thinking, and cultural awareness. She authored several reports on airport security, and she pushed the Commission to change funding contracts to make attention to gender diversity a requirement. At the time, she explains,

> *There was no consideration given to people's experience of security. . . . If you have ten white men and two white women from rich European countries sitting around a table deciding whether something is appropriate of not, you have very little insight into people who are not in that cohort. There was no understanding that it might not work that well for a woman, a Black person. There was very little understanding of people who live in countries where security is not your safety net. . . . For rich western societies, security is comfort and safety; for not rich, non-western people security can mean oppression and fear. There is a fine line between security as safety and security as oppression.* (interview 2020)

However, as the years went by, it became harder for her to celebrate efforts to temper power or isolate herself from the more grotesque experiments masquerading as research.

In the United States, debates over policing, at least since the 1960s, have turned on whether the institution is reformable or if we should dismantle it in favor of something new. The societal investment in safety and security is, as we have shown in this book, an important barrier to real change, but in the professional realm of security, the very same question is being asked: Is it possible to reform security institutions, or should they be dismantled in favor of something new, if, that is, we can imagine an alternative future? Sarah's ethnographic story is important here because it follows an illustrative arc from insider to activist. She searched for answers to uncomfortable questions and discovered that the power to make meaningful societal change is not where one expects it to be.

Mark spoke at a counterterrorism conference hosted by Sarah in 2017 (at that point, INDECT was still a source of embarrassment). The event was organized in the febrile period after the ISIS attacks on the *Charlie Hebdo* office, the Bataclan, and Brussels Airport. Conference attendees were oddly unruffled by terrorist atrocities. They were, however, energized by the opportunities presented by counterterrorism—surveillance cameras would be needed, along with biometric identification, greater border control, and the fortification of airports.

During an early morning panel discussion between industrial representatives, the accuracy of predictive security systems was discussed. Police and frontline emergency workers attempted to intervene in the discussion to point to the moderate threat level, but the academics and technologists dismissed the views of these "end users." Sarah, however, proved to be a more formidable critic. She understood the technical systems, the pseudo-scientific theories of risk, and the historical trend data on terrorism. "This is just technological solutionism," she said again and again. She remembers thinking, "It is not possible to stop every threat, but they want to put cling-film around Europe, to baby-proof Europe," and sell people the cling-film at a high price (interview 2021). The event ended with a keynote address from a well-known politician, a former minister for justice turned security lobbyist. Sarah gave the concluding remarks. Instead of delivering a diplomatic summation, she berated the workshop attendees for failing to protect human rights, before turning on the former politician for his support for "hang 'em high" counterterrorism legislation. But the politician, angered, struck back, hands raised as if surrendering, with,

> *You think we're the problem? The people here? I was a justice minister for ten years. My phone rang day and night. The people, your nice friends and neighbors, demanding law and order, an end to this and that. Children, terrorists, everyone to be locked up. If I listened to my voters, there'd be someone hanging from every lamppost in the country. I was holding back the forces of darkness with my moderation!*

This was the last time that Sarah hosted a policy or networking event. She stepped back from the security sector. She gives several reasons, personal and professional, but the truth is mundane. After 9/11, the security sector needed energetic entrepreneurs and brokers, but over time the bureaucracy, accounting requirements, and reporting demands pushed out the charismatic actors in favor of larger operators. Sarah became a figure of a moment in time. However, we should attend to her ethnographic story because it explodes the powerful myths that still sustain the EU security-industrial complex, namely (1) that so-called internal security is separate from the defense sector, and by extension the arms industry; (2) that internal security is a scientific and empirical policy project as opposed to a commercial and opportunistic one propelled by fear; and (3) that the vast expenditure on security is ultimately for the benefit of society. Our tracking of Sarah's career here shows that EU homeland security is imbricated with an older military-industrial complex, and that it must be understood as an extractive form of security capitalism. Immediately, questions of reform, or radical change, come to mind. And so, we must consider the benefit to society of continuing with the way things are, asking who benefits here?

Immediately after 9/11, securitization was deemed to be necessary, good even, and objections were signs of weakness, treason even. However, we now have a reasonably full accounting of the Global War on Terror, and the balance sheet shows shocking human costs and an enormous moral debt. During the twenty years from 2001 to 2021, the US government spent between $6 and $8 trillion on invasions, surveillance, and efforts to shadowbox with elusive enemies. Brown University's Costs of War project estimates that over three hundred thousand civilians may have died from war-related violence in Iraq, Afghanistan, and neighboring Pakistan, just three of the countries directly affected. Thirty-eight million people were displaced from their homes; fifty countries were implicated in "extraordinary rendition," and well over one hundred countries pushed through counterterror legislation that criminalized dissidents, activists, and artists. Two decades later, the costs continue to mount. The murderous cult that is ISIS emerged in the ruins of Iraq, neighboring Syria collapsed in flames, and after twenty years of "progress," Afghanistan was hastily abandoned to Taliban rule. The EU played a role in all of this, with many countries featuring on the map of rendition "black sites" and with most EU states sending troops to Afghanistan. If there was a benefit from any of this, it is hard to see.

During the early days of the War on Terror, security sector insiders, including Sarah, argued that the number of failed and foiled terror plots indicated the effectiveness of counterterror measures. However, as time went on, it became clear that evidence in support of the effectiveness of anti-terror measures was lacking. In 2015, for example, experimental assessments of US airports showed that the Department of Homeland Security's Transportation Security Administration (TSA) counterterror measures were 95 percent ineffective. When the same assessments were conducted two years later, there was little improvement to report. Indeed, the DHS inspector general's reports on counterterrorism have been so critical of the TSA that the agency has sought to have them classified to avoid public scrutiny.

The European security-industrial complex apes its American cousin, so it suffers the same expensive failure with a slight delay. Just like the United States, in the European security sector failure is rarely punished. The absence of penalties springs partly from a broad agreement on core ideas among sectoral insiders. Interestingly, Sarah and her counterparts were always critical of US actions in Iraq and Afghanistan—in Europe, an anti-American posture is still fashionable among intellectuals—but they accepted that military operations and drone strikes were part and parcel of modern geopolitics. Once one accepts that preemptive extrajudicial assassination is part of the unpleasant business of counterterrorism—sometimes referred to as "mowing the lawn," to borrow the Israeli phrase—then one's attendance at security exhibitions of Leclerc tanks and fighter jets is merely a business trip. And yet, when the security boomerang returned to hit middle-class Europe in the form of INDECT, distant theoretical matters became immediate, troubling, and intolerable. There is an important lesson here.

Sarah once said, "There is a fine line between security as safety and security as oppression." Ordinary members of society, nice friends and neighbors, demand security as safety. Those ordinary members of society will tolerate oppression for others so long as it means safety for them. Security capitalism in America, Europe, and elsewhere, has found a rich and powerful market for its fear-based products. Security as oppression is visited on the poor, the marginal, and the children incinerated by European weapons in faraway Yemen. What to do?

We can, and we will, protest the next war, and we will protest any expansion of mass surveillance, but we all must realize that the opportunity to protest is closer than we think. Right now, the Pentagon is investing in the next generation of weapons, trying to crack the code of cyberwar by investing in quantum computing and AI. Brussels is blessing the rearmament of Europe on the pretext of defending the freedom of Ukraine. These investments are made in your city. They require your university's campus and its graduates. For many people, the war in Afghanistan seemed theoretical, something taking place over the horizon. It was also cast as a humanitarian intervention. Rory Stewart and Gerald Knaus give a portrait of the typical foreign worker in Afghanistan: credentialed, hardworking, but with "little knowledge of Afghan archaeology, anthropology, geography, history, language, literature or theology," and gone after a year to the next job with a new line on their CV.[5] An alert and knowledgeable citizen would never have assumed that the Afghan government would facilitate a flowering of gender equality and democratic representation. History, very recent history, explains why. Following the US overthrow of the Taliban, a new government was installed, and 60 percent of the provincial governors appointed were former warlords, and forty warlords and twenty-four criminal gang leaders entered parliament—their first act was to pass an amnesty for past war crimes. In short, our universities are places where defunding can begin, meaning acting against the hard-power machinery of security capitalism and paying critical attention to culturally inattentive and materially complicit forms of soft power. To defund Homeland Security in Europe is just as straightforward. Each year, the security sector grows because universities, police forces, armies, and emergency managers are not held to account for their participation. If we focus on homeland security, we may be able to separate the desire for safety among ordinary members of society from the willingness to oppress others.

Reclaiming homeland security, then, means breaking out of a pattern of behavior by reimagining public safety without oppression. Otherwise, the pattern continues, real change never happens, and as T. S. Eliot reminds us in *Murder in the Cathedral,*

> We do not know very much of the future
> Except that from generation to generation
> The same things happen again and again. . . .
> Sever the cord, shed the scale. Only
> The fool, fixed in his folly, may think
> He can turn the wheel on which he turns.

CONCLUSION: DEFUND SECURITY

Institutions develop over time ostensibly to serve the public good. When institutions fail to do so, and public trust is lost, responsible societies must reform them or, if need be, abolish them entirely. History shows significant institutional changes have occurred in each area addressed in this book. Today, gated communities pockmark suburban America. However, the United States once led the world in urban planning for the public good, and there is no reason this cannot happen again. Societies have reimagined failed police institutions, such as in the case of Northern Ireland mentioned in this book. The same applies to international security institutions. Historically, enemies have come and gone, and states have removed their physical, psychological, and institutional fortifications accordingly.

In 2020, antiracism protests burned through American cities and sparked protests worldwide. Protesters made a seemingly new demand, Defund the Police. The political establishment dismissed the demand as unrealistic, perhaps even a recipe for anarchy from the pages of some radical cookbook. However, those who looked beyond the snappy slogan were confronted with several utterly reasonable questions. Do the police serve the public? If not, why not reduce the funding allocated to their already bloated budgets and invest in public safety, youth services, education, and healthcare? (Why not stop the so-called Pentagon Pipeline from pumping weapons of war into local communities? After all, many small and relatively safe US cities now possess mine-resistant armored personnel vehicles, and it is entirely unclear why university campus police require M-16s.) Here we argue that an agenda that strives for real equality and justice must grapple with the problem of security.

In *Trapped*, we have shown that gated suburban communities threaten societal functioning by sucking in societal resources and spewing out segregation and suspicion. We have shown that fortified urban enclaves exacerbate inequality and redirect scarce public resources to corporations and cosmopolitan elites. We have shown that security capitalism precedes, surrounds, and strangles policing, turning public safety into a marketplace for bad ideas and ineffective gadgets. Counterterrorism and homeland security now act in the interests of the security-industrial complex, not public safety. The question is this: What steps might we take to defund security? Here we offer five suggestions.

1. OPEN THE GATES

People who purchase homes in gated suburban communities are motivated, in large part, by fear. They say they are fleeing criminality, and many are, but they also reveal a desire to pull away from everyday risk and the noisy chaos of social relations. Gated suburban communities promise a life with other "nice" (read middle-class or white) people like themselves. They buy security, and segregation comes with the package. Of course, the promise of a risk-free life with like-minded neighbors is false on two levels. Gated suburban communities are no safer than others, yet uncomfortable "fear talk" saturates interior life in a secured enclave. The fear talk is often about the workers who operate the community daily, showing that the promise of security is empty on another level. Not only is the interior world dependent on labor and other support from the outside, but the interior of security capitalism is inherently extractive. The gated community diverts resources, contributes to racialized segregation, and compounds societal fracturing, all of which amplifies the perceived need for security.

The only way out of the security trap is to reintegrate gated communities. To do this, we must focus on the systems that enable them. Wealthy and middle-class people who wish to reside in gated communities are screened for financial well-being and social acceptability by homeowners' associations (HOAs) and common interest developments (CIDs). These structures have no moral basis;

they have no fixed political basis; they are the tools of segregation by securitization. There is a clear political argument for removing these structures.

2. TAKE BACK THE CITY

Fortified enclaves have mushroomed in cities worldwide. Whereas many enclaves for the elite promote themselves as separate and securitized, New York's trendy Hudson Yards was packaged as an opportunity for urban renewal. Instead, we have an island of expensive residences, restaurants, and designer shops, patrolled by black-clad security guards, and set within a forest of surveillance cameras. There is little doubt that, like gated suburban developments, residents of Hudson Yards know their desire for security contributes to social segregation. However, their fears and desires are outcomes of decades of hard-to-undo social programming. What we can undo is the system that produced Hudson Yards in the first place, a system which refuses to acknowledge any alternative.

The story of Hudson Yards is a chapter in the financialization of New York. The city was driven to near bankruptcy in the 1970s. Private interests stepped in, and later investors appeared as saviors prepared to take risks. Private enclaves built for "the right kind of people" ensured a low-risk and profitable return on investment. This protected class wants security, a package of ideas, gadgets, and anti-social designs that double as the building blocks of contemporary segregation. Meaningful change will only come if we persuade people that there is an alternative to Hudson Yards. There are examples of equitable development, and we must push for more projects in the public interest before security traps us all.

3. REIMAGINE POLICING

Numerous societies worldwide have tried and failed to reform their police. In 1968, the US National Advisory Commission on Civil Disorders linked police violence to systemic racism and civil unrest. However, the establishment lacked the will to push through meaningful changes. As Maya Angelou remembers, each subsequent act of police violence provoked a "nightmarish sense of déjà vu," and each protest appeared as a "rehearsal for the next rehearsal."[1] Today, reform of dysfunctional law enforcement institutions, from the London Metropolitan Police to the Minneapolis Police Department, seems just as elusive. However, there is hope.

As we showed in this book, there is a good understanding of the kinds of policing tactics that work and those that do not, and there are examples where deep institutional transformations have occurred. However, contrary to other scholarly statements on reimagining policing, here we have not limited our discussion to the institution of policing, as if that represents a whole world. Instead, we point to how security capitalism now surrounds and infests law enforcement, from private security services to transformed public institutions. To reimagine policing, we must remove barriers to the imagination, and security is one of the highest barriers. To borrow again from Angela Davis, we must persuade people that "safety, safeguarded by violence, is not really safety."[2]

In this book, we argued that public safety is being outsourced to security capitalist interests. People are living in gated suburban neighborhoods and in exclusionary urban enclaves. Increasingly, security guards resolve matters of public safety. The cameras in your neighborhood are plugged into a vast and still-growing security-industrial complex. Meaningful and lasting change will not come from reforming bad examples of policing, because the desire for security is pushing in the opposite direction. Here we are arguing that by removing security capitalism from the arena of public safety we will increase the possibility of meaningful change.

4. COUNTER COUNTERTERRORISM

Throughout history, empires and states have bled resources fighting real and imagined terrorists, from Roman efforts to crush Jewish Zealots to Vietnam-era efforts to destroy the Ho Chi Minh trail. During the past two decades, the US government spent approximately $7 trillion destabilizing the Middle East in the name of counterterrorism, resulting in at least three hundred thousand civilian deaths. However, the number of deaths per annum from terrorism is higher than in 2001. Although counterterrorism has slipped from the agenda of Western governments in today's era of renewed great power competition, the anti-terror systems, processes, and personnel put in place after 9/11 remain, and the longer they remain, the more they will be regarded as regular features of life. As Graham Greene wrote in *The Quiet American*, the passage of time, "the scratches of feet and the erosion of weather," can make the most preposterous fabrication look convincing.[3]

How might we counter counterterrorism? One might focus on Western military adventures, the cooption of anti-terror discourse by authoritarians, or the current strategy to conduct murderous operations "over the horizon." This book focused on the contemporary airport, counterterrorism's preferred laboratory for experiments in costly security measures. The airport is also a lightning rod for societal fear of terrorism, where the public accepts costly and intrusive measures despite their inefficacy. How do we convince people that airport security is not a necessary stage in a middle-class adventure but, instead, a space one pays to have one's liberty stripped off and replaced with illusionary safety? This book showed that behind counterterrorism's secrecy, gadgetry, and performative seriousness, we find rather ordinary men and women working, often problematically, to guarantee public safety. Those who operate the airport quietly are the bedrock of public safety. They will still stand tomorrow if we rid ourselves of unnecessary and ineffective measures today.

Throughout *Trapped*, we have shown that security capitalism relies on investors, the middle-class people who believe they have nothing to hide and nothing to fear.

We must remind people that security is to be feared and show them that it operates by claiming to master our fears for us. To counter counterterrorism effectively, we must expose this fake mastery. Our university campuses are where the pseudo-science of counter-radicalization is gaining convincingness. Intelligence studies, homeland security studies, and myriad neighboring activities can and should be defunded.

5. RECLAIM THE HOMELAND

In his farewell address, President Dwight D. Eisenhower warned us that security capitalism had escaped the confines of the defense sector and was assaulting "the very structure of society." However, he still hoped that an "alert and knowledgeable citizenry" would stand firm, and he identified the "free university" as a likely battleground. During the Vietnam era, many universities listened to antiwar protestors and suspended their ties with the Pentagon. Security and defense research flourished in quasi-private federally funded research and development centers (FFRDCs), such as the famous RAND Corporation and MIT's Lincoln Lab. In many cases, however, the university campus was divided. For example, Stanford University students have long protested military recruiters on campus. However, they protest in the shadow of the Hoover Tower, the think tank where Director Condoleezza Rice hosts research fellows and visiting authoritarians.

In the wake of 9/11, many universities strengthened their relationship with the security-industrial complex, rallying to defend the "homeland." Today, the Department of Homeland Security openly operates centers of excellence in multiple universities, from the Soft-Target Engineering Center at Northeastern University to the Criminal Investigations Center at George Mason University. It also convenes an Academic Partnership Council to recruit the education sector in the fight against terrorism, while providing training opportunities for the security sector's workforce.

The War on Terror is yesterday's conflict, so the demand for academic adjacency has shifted to new fields such as artificial intelligence (AI), where defense sector staff are increasing their campus footprint to prepare for future hybrid wars. When challenged about these partnerships, universities claim no direct defense link and no dual-use manufacturing. However, this is precisely the false distinction that we seek to challenge. Whereas we once protested the presence of the military-industrial complex, uniformed soldiers, and shadowy intelligence agency staff, we must now protest the unwarranted influence of the more nebulous security-industrial complex. Success would mean less global violence, less mass surveillance, and better approaches to problems such as policing and foreign policy. There are also significant ancillary benefits. For example, the Pentagon is the largest institutional consumer of petroleum on planet Earth. If we defund the security-industrial complex, we can massively reduce an unnecessary carbon boot print.

Of course, it is relatively easy to protest outside a building that houses defense research or to stand in the shadow of Stanford's Hoover Tower to decry the toxic foreign policy brewed there. It is harder to confront well-meaning colleagues who believe military adventures help spread democracy and gender equality. For two decades, the US propped up a Potemkin state in Afghanistan. Aid agencies, technocrats on sabbatical, and applied academics all played a supporting role. Perhaps unsurprisingly, in its final years, the Kabul government resembled a dysfunctional faculty committee. Everyone seemed to have a graduate degree from a foreign university, and President Ghani regularly quoted sources from his PhD in anthropology from Columbia University. All was well until the country collapsed. In this light, it is shocking that a recent critique of US warfighting demanded greater inclusion of "political science, development studies, public health, International Relations, history, ethics and philosophy, among other disciplines."[4]

Around the world, from Palestine to São Paulo, universities have long been spaces where people contest security. In Europe, campuses have been quiet on this issue, though things will likely change. During the past decade, the EU quietly established structures to advance the so-called Security Union, such as the Permanent Structured Cooperation (PESCO) of militaries and the European Defense Fund (EDF). The Russian invasion of Ukraine is justifying ever-greater bellicosity. In March 2022, EU heads of state issued the so-called Strategic

Compass committing member states to increase security expenditure. Germany is talking of a *Zeitenwende*, a turning point whereby their pleasingly noiseless and efficient security sector will assume a more significant role in public life. Universities, as Eisenhower foresaw, are now battlegrounds. A civil clause constitutionally prohibits many German universities from participating in defense research. Until recently, "pacificist" was not an insult in Germany. The fight to reclaim homeland security may take place very close to home.

Today, as activists and academics call for a reimagining of policing, there is much we can and should do to help. We can draw on comparative ethnographic examples to evaluate modern policing, but those examples show an institution surrounded and infested by security capitalism. Transforming policing, then, involves attending to security. We encourage attention to the security-industrial complex and other sites where security capitalism is flourishing. We must also hold the middle classes and mainstream institutions like universities accountable. Security is everywhere these days; thus, it is everyone's problem. The challenge is to open our societal gates, reclaim our cities, and counter securitization wherever we find it. We are trapped by security, and we must help each other escape.

ACKNOWLEDGMENTS

Setha would like to thank her husband, Joel Lefkowitz, and sister, Anna Harwin, for their wisdom about fear and social justice. Mark is grateful to his wife, Eileen, and to his baby, Sean, who successfully turned two years old during the writing of this book.

This book began life as a sketch on a napkin. We found that we shared a concern with the growing intrusion of security into many aspects of contemporary life, and we noted that the scholarly literature did not yet explore the middle-class complicity with—perhaps even love of—security. At a conference in Germany, we sketched out a book on a napkin that would address itself to the middle classes and the wealthy, a book that would argue that change was possible.

To ground our perspectives on security, we decided to give the reader a detailed and characterful account of matters such as residential and counterterror security. To protect anonymity and privacy, we use pseudonyms throughout the book and disguise people's identities further by describing composite characters and events. We are sure that none of the people we worked with will dispute the facts in our descriptions, though some will disagree with our conclusions. We openly shared our dissatisfaction with the state of security today. So did our research participants. This book emerged from our shared sense that something is profoundly wrong and that there is much to change.

Mark acknowledges the generous support of his ethnographic research by the Global Foresight project funded by the Riksbankens Jubileumsfond.

Numerous foundations and granting agencies provided the financial support for Setha's ethnographic fieldwork. The writing of this book was funded by a series of generous fellowships from the Center for the Future of Places directed by Tigran Haas at KTH in Stockholm with funding from Peter Elmlund of the Ax:son Johnson Foundation. The gated community research was funded by the Wenner-Gren Foundation for Anthropological Research and the Research Foundation of the City University of New York. The Russell Sage Foundation funded a pilot study of Battery Park City community changes post-9/11. Setha would like to thank the many foundations that made these projects possible and the Graduate Center of the City University of New York for funding sabbatical leaves and allowing her take release time so that she could complete the fieldwork and write up the findings.

A long list of graduate students at the Graduate Center of CUNY collected data used in this book. Many of the ethnographic projects were undertaken by research teams that were part of the Public Space Research Group. The Battery Park City project included Mike Lamb and Dana Taplin whom Setha continues to work with. The gated community co-researchers—Elena Danaila, Andrew Kirby, Lynmari Benitez, and Mariana Diaz-Wionczek—were graduate students at the time and collected many of the New York City interviews. The Tompkins Square Park study was part of the Ethnography of Space and Place course and Merrit Corrigan, Bengi Sullu, Anthony Ramos, and Elisandro Garza contributed their fieldnotes, maps, interviews, and many insights. Setha is grateful to these young scholars who made the research process fun and compelling. Their ideas, enthusiasm, and hard work kept projects going even when faced with adversity and setbacks—she could not have completed this work without them, and it would not have been as meaningful or fulfilling.

NOTES

1. This extract from a recorded conversation is one of fourteen such interviews with survivors of the terror attack in the upper car park area of the mall. The interview was part of an empirical study of public behavior during the first minutes of terrorist attacks in France, the UK, Ireland, and Kenya directed by Mark Maguire. See Mark Maguire and David A. Westbrook, *Getting through Security: Counterterrorism, Bureaucracy, and a Sense of the Modern* (London and New York: Routledge, 2020).

2. Of course, there are exceptions, and our ethnographic work acknowledges an important strand of Marxist political philosophy. See George S. Rigakos, *Security/Capital: A General Theory of Pacification* (Edinburgh: Edinburgh University Press, 2016); also Mark Neocleous, *Critique of Security* (Edinburgh: Edinburgh University Press, 2008). However, following Michel Foucault, we also acknowledge that contemporary security does not seek total discipline or attempt to entirely remake the reality to which it responds, see Mark Maguire and Pete Fussey, "Sensing Evil: Counterterrorism, Techno-science, and the Cul-

tural Reproduction of Security," *Focaal: Journal of Global and Historical Anthropology* 75, no. 3 (2016): 31–44.

3. Scholars who write about areas such as policy, technology implementation, and surveillance often assume that security is a techno-social process in a dialectic relationship with insecurity (or uncertainty). Academics and technologists thus practice different kinds of "solutionism." However, in the areas we write about in this book, for example urban fortification and counterterrorism, research participants reveal (usually immediately) that security stands in opposition to chaos, variously defined. This is a key, and understudied, source of power and legitimacy for security capitalism—people will live with insecurity, or uncertainty, but are reluctant to yield to what they see as the forces of chaos.

INTRODUCTION

1. Throughout *Trapped* we discuss public safety and the public interest. We are cognizant that "the public" is a product of self-identification, imagination, and governmentality. There are ambiguities and contradictions plated into the idea, and "counter-publics" may be more than opposition to exclusionary mainstream political culture. However, rather than constantly caveat every statement on public matters, we acknowledge that it is an essentially contested concept, see Michael Warner, *Publics and Counter-publics* (New York: Zone Books, 2002).

2. See Alex S. Vitale, *The End of Police* (New York and London: Verso, 2017).

3. See Angela Davis, "Freedom Struggle." *Democracy Now.* September 7, 2020. https://www.democracynow.org/2020/9/7/freedom_struggle_angela_davis_on_calls.

4. See Thomas Hobbes, *Leviathan* (Oxford: Clarendon Press, [1651] 1909.). Some may object here: surely this appeal to

Western philosophy, with its obsessive attention to states, war, and security is a limiting gesture? Yes, the "canon" is indeed limited. And yet all societies attempt to resolve the problem of security in some way, enlisting myriad resources between the individual's strength and the nation's army. Adventurous searches for security done differently—the romantic gesture mocked by Nietzsche—show few transferrable ideas. We are keen to look for alternatives in the contemporary.

5. Jean-Jacques Rousseau, *A Discourse on Inequality* (New York: The Philosophical Library, 2016), 63.

6. Karl Marx, "On the Jewish Question" (1843), in *The Marx-Engels Reader,* ed. Robert Tucker, 26–46 (New York: Norton & Co., 1978), 43.

7. Radical Black scholars have for a long time noted that the institution we call the police is historically and culturally contingent. See, for example, Terry Jones, "The Police in America: A Black Viewpoint," *The Black Scholar* 9, no. 2 (1977): 22–31, 36–39. If the institution is contingent, they argue, then it can be made anew. But it is only recently that activists such as Angela Davis have pointed to the institutional provision of security as a critical dimension to this project.

8. Shoshana Zuboff, *The Age of Surveillance Capitalism: The Fight for a Human Future at the New Frontier of Power* (New York and London: Profile Books, 2019).

9. See Yasha Levine, *Surveillance Valley: The Secret Military History of the Internet* (New York and London: Public Affairs, 2018).

10. Setha Low and Mark Maguire, eds., *Spaces of Security: Ethnographies of Security-scapes, Surveillance, and Control* (New York: New York University Press, 2019).

11. Peter Sloterdijk, *In the World Interior of Capital: Towards a Philosophical Theory of Globalization* (London and New York: Polity Press, 2013).

12. Anthropologists are showing a renewed interest in traps and "entrapment" (for an excellent example see Alberto Corsín Jiménez and Chloe Nahum-Claudel, "The Anthropology of Traps: Concrete Technologies and Theoretical Interfaces." *Journal of Material Culture* 24, no. 4 (2019): 383–400). Entrapment, as we have shown elsewhere, is logically entailed in security, and discussion of it should be sufficiently specific to illuminate that domain. See Mark Maguire and David A. Westbrook, *Getting through Security: Counterterrorism, Bureaucracy, and a Sense of the Modern* (London and New York: Routledge, 2020).

13. See Rob Flynn and Paul Bellaby, *Risk and the Public Acceptance of New Technologies* (London: Palgrave Macmillan, 2007).

CHAPTER 1

1. Mara Gay, "To Cut New York Housing Costs, Ease Suburb's Zoning Laws," *New York Times*, Opinion. February 23, 2023, A22. Richard Kahlenberg, *Excluded: How Snob Zoning, Nimbyism, and Class Bias Build the Walls We Don't See* (New York: Public Affairs, 2023).

2. Elena Danaila and Setha Low were the interviewers at Manor House.

3. Pseudonyms are used for the interviewees.

4. Manor House is a fictitious name for the gated development. The use of the term *manor* references the manor house that originally was on the property.

5. David M. P. Freund, *Colored Property: State Policy and White Racial Politics in Suburban America* (Chicago: University Chicago Press, 2007); Richard Rothstein, *The Color of Law: A Forgotten History of How Our Government Segregated America* (New York: W. W. Norton, 2017).

6. Setha Low, *Behind the Gates: Life, Security, and the Pursuit of Happiness in Fortress America* (New York: Routledge,

2003); Robert L. Lang and K. A. Danielson, "Gated Communities in America," *Housing Policy Debate* 8, no. 4 (1997): 867–899; Tom Sanchez and Robert L. Lang, "Security versus Status: The Two Worlds of Gated Communities," *Census Note 02:02* (Alexandria: Metropolitan Institute at Virginia Tech, 2002); *Gated Community Data*, Las Vegas, Nevada, https://gatedcommunitynews.com/gated-community-data.

7. Amy Gamerman, "The New Gated Community: More Land, Fewer Neighbors," *Wall Street Journal*, August 24, 2017. https://www.wssj.com/articles/the-new-gated-community-more-land-fewer-neighbors-1503579674?tesla=y.

8. Renaud Le Goix and Elena Vesselinow, "Inequality Shaping Processes and Gated Communities in the US Western Metropolitan Areas," *Urban Studies* 52 (2015): 619–638.

9. Wendy Brown, *Walled States, Waning Sovereignty* (New York: Zone Books, 2010).

10. Stephen Graham and Simon Marvin, *Splintering Urbanism: Networked Infrastructures, Technological Mobilities, and the Urban Condition* (London: Routledge, 2001).

11. Octavia Butler, *Parable of the Sower* (New York: Grand Central Publishing, [1998] 2019).

12. Michalis Lianos, "Social Control after Foucault," *Surveillance & Society* 1, no. 3 (2003): 412–430.

13. Brown, *Walled States, Waning Sovereignty*, 41.

14. Setha Low, "Towards a Theory of Urban Fragmentation: A Cross-Cultural Analysis of Fear, Privatization, and the State," *Cybergeo: Revue européenne de géographie*, Article 349, October 2, 2006.

CONCEPT NOTE: INTERIOR LIFE

1. See Ayn Rand, *Atlas Shrugged* (New York: Dutton, 1957); with more precision in Ayn Rand, *For the New Intellectual* (New York: Signet, 1963), 695.

2. Setha Low and Mark Maguire, eds., *Spaces of Security: Ethnographies of Security-scapes, Surveillance, and Control* (New York: New York University Press, 2019).

3. Peter Sloterdijk, *In the World Interior of Capital: Towards a Philosophical Theory of Globalization* (London and New York: Polity Press, 2013), 213.

CHAPTER 2

1. Michael Kimmelman, "Hudson Yards Is Manhattan's Biggest, Newest, Slickest Gated Community: Is This the Neighborhood New York Deserves?" *New York Times*, March 14, 2019; Sharon Mattern, "Instrumental City: The View from Hudson Yards, circa 2019," *Places*. April 2016.

2. Julian Brash, *Bloomberg's New York: Class and Governance in the Luxury City* (Athens: University of Georgia Press, 2011).

3. Setha Low, *Why Public Space Matters* (New York and London: Oxford University Press, 2023); Troy Simpson, "Open to the Public(s): A Critical Examination of Public Space in the Smart City." Dissertation proposal (updated), environmental psychology (The Graduate Center, City University of New York, [2019] 2022).

4. Interview with Mr. Ross as reported in Kimmelman, "Hudson Yards Is Manhattan's Biggest, Newest, Slickest Gated Community."

5. Katherine Clarke, "The Luxury Tower Built for New York's Elite Still Sits Half Empty," *Wall Street Journal,* July 13, 2023. https://www.wsj.com/articles/hudson-yards-condos.

6. Don Mitchell and Lynn A. Staeheli, "Clean and Safe? Property Redevelopment, Public Space, and Homelessness in Downtown San Diego," in *The Politics of Public Space,* ed. Setha Low and Neil Smith, 143–175 (New York: Routledge, 2005).

7. Setha Low, *Behind the Gates: Life, Security, and the Pursuit of Happiness in Fortress America* (New York: Routledge, 2003).

8. David L. Altheide, "Notes towards a Politics of Fear," *Journal for Crime, Conflict and the Media* 1, no. 1 (2003): 37–54.

9. Joseph Masco, *The Theater of Operations* (Durham, NC: Duke University Press, 2014).

10. Saskia Sassen, *The Global City: New York, London, Tokyo* (Princeton, NJ: Princeton University Press, 2001).

11. Emil Røyrvik, "The Sociality of Securitization: Symbolic Weapons of Mass Deception," *iNtergraph* 2, no. 2 (2010): 1–14.

12. Suleiman Osman, "'We're Doing It Ourselves': The Unexpected Origins of New York City's Public-Private Parks during the 1970s Fiscal Crisis," *Journal of Planning History* 16, no. 30 (2017): 162–174.

13. Kevin Ward, "Creating a Personality for Downtown: Business Improvement Districts in Milwaukee," *Urban Geography* 28, no. 8 (2007): 781–808; M. Steel and M. Symes, "The Privatization of Public Space? The American Experience of Business Improvement Districts and Their Relationship to Local Governance," *Local Government Studies* 31, no. 3 (2005): 321–334.

14. Jeremy Kayden, *Privately Owned Public Space: The New York Experience* (New York: Wiley, 2000).

15. Jeremy Nemeth, "Lost Space: Security Zones and New York City's Shrinking Public Space," *International Journal of Urban and Regional Research* 34, no. 1 (2010): 20–34.

16. Greg Smithsimon, "Dispersing the Crowd: Bonus Plazas and the Creation of Public Space," *Urban Affairs Review* 43, no. 3 (2008): 325–351.

17. Urvashi Uberoy and Keith Collins, "New Yorkers Got Broken Promises. Developers Got 20 Million Sq. Ft.," *New York Times*, July 21, 2023, https://www.nytimes.com/interactive/2023/07/21/nyregion/nyc-developers-private-owned.

18. POPS are a good deal for developers making up 3.8 million square feet of ostensibly public space, while gaining 20.7 million square feet of bonus space.

19. Setha Low and Zoltan Gluck, "A Sociospatial Framework for the Anthropology of Security," *Anthropology Theory* 17, no. 3 (2017): 281–296.

20. Zoltan Gluck, "Security Urbanism and the Counterterror State of Kenya," *Anthropological Theory* 17, no. 3 (2017): 297–321.

21. Mona Fawaz, Mona Harb, and Ahmad Gharbieh, "Living Beirut's Security Zones: An Investigation of the Modalities and Practice of Urban Security," *City & Society* 24, no. 2 (2012): 173–195.

22. The EB-5 program was designed to allow foreign investors to gain permanent residence (a "green card") in the United States. It requires a minimum investment of $1 million, or $500,000 if the investment is in a rural or targeted high-unemployment area where unemployment is 150 percent of the national average. The investment also must result in the creation of at least ten jobs.

23. T. Simpson, "Public Space in the Smart City: Navigating the Ambiguities of Emerging Digital Infrastructure" (presentation). The Public Space Research Group, Network Event, November 12, 2021.

24. John Allen, "Berlin's Potsdamer Platz and the Seductive Logic of Public Spaces," *Urban Studies* 43, no. 2 (2006): 441–455.

25. Excerpts of interviews from Simpson, "Public Space in the Smart City."

26. Simpson, "Open to the Public(s)"; Brash, *Bloomberg's New York.*

27. Excerpts of interviews from Simpson, "Public Space in the Smart City."

28. Peter Adey, Laure Brayer, Damien Masson, Patrick Murphy, Paul Simpson, and Nicolas Tixier, "Pour votre tranquillite: Ambiance, Atmosphere, and Surveillance," *Geoforum* 49 (2013): 299–309.

29. Elizabeth Seaton, "The Commodification of Fear," *Topias* 5 (2018): 1–19.

30. Chris Gilliard, "The Rise of 'Luxury Surveillance,'" *The Atlantic*, October 18, 2022. https://www.theatlantic.com/technology/archive/2022/10/amazon.

CONCEPT NOTE: SECURITY CAPITALISM

1. Karl Marx, "On the Jewish Question" (1843), in *The Marx-Engels Reader*, 2nd ed., ed. Robert C. Tucker (London and New York: W. W. Norton and Co., 1978), 43–44 passim. Political philosophers extend Marx's work by exploring security as "pacification." See George S. Rigakos, *Security/Capital: A General Theory of Pacification* (Edinburgh: Edinburgh University Press, 2016); Mark Neocleous, *Critique of Security* (Edinburgh: Edinburgh University Press, 2008).

CHAPTER 3

1. Divisions in Ireland run deep and show many fault lines. Historians view the so-called Troubles as a period when minority Catholic citizens in Northern Ireland demanded equal civil rights from the majority-Protestant and British-backed regional government. This political movement was captured by more aggressive Catholic nationalism as expressed by the Provisional Irish Republican Army (IRA) and the Sinn Féin party. The stated aim of the IRA and Sinn Féin is an end to British colonialism and a United Ireland. The more aggressive elements of Northern Irish Protestantism congealed into Loyalist paramilitary groups such as the Ulster Volunteer Force (UVF). However, this picture is painted with broad brush strokes: Northern Ireland is striated by class differences and home to surprising political and viewpoint diversity.

2. William Butler Yeats, "Remorse for Intemperate Speech," in *The Winding Stair and Other Poems* (London: Scribner, [1933] 2011), 47.

3. Frederick Engels, "Letter to Karl Marx, 25 May 1853," in *Karl Marx and Frederick Engels: Ireland and the Irish Question* (Moscow: Progress Publishers, 1971), 93.

4. A more insightful account of policing in Ireland is available in Alexis de Tocqueville's account of this 1835 tour of the country accompanied by Gustave de Beaumont; see Alexis de Tocqueville, *Journeys to Ireland and England*, ed. J. P. Meyer, trans. George Lawrence and J. P. Mayer (New Haven, CT: Yale University Press, 1958).

5. These words are from a speech by the first commissioner of the post-independence Civic Guard, the forerunner of the Garda Síochána. Records of speeches are not transcripts and can thus be inaccurate. This quotation is taken from Vicky Conway, *Policing Twentieth Century Ireland: A History of An Garda Síochána* (London and New York: Routledge, 2014).

6. Anthropologist Didier Fassin describes the stop-and-frisk policing of youth in Parisian banlieues. According to Fassin, youths are subjected to "rituals of mortification" by police, and they "internalize" these humiliations, learning that police are not to be trusted. However, compelling though this analysis seems, the process is more complicated than he suspects, and the potential outcome is far more dangerous. Humiliation by police (or military) tends to produce individual-level inertia. However, if one is witness to the humiliation of a close friend or family member the effect is moral outrage and often violent rage. See Didier Fassin, *Enforcing Order: An Ethnography of Urban Policing* (Cambridge: Polity Press, 2013); cf. Jeremy Ginges and Scott Atran, "Humiliation and the Inertia Effect: Implications for Understanding Violence and Compromise in Intractable Intergroup Conflicts," *Journal of Cognition and Culture* 8, nos. 3/4 (2008): 281–294.

7. See Martin Van Creveld, *The Transformation of War* (London and New York: The Free Press, 1991), 207. With the rise of hybrid warfare, and the prominent role played by private military companies like the Wagner Group, one may argue that the Russian state has followed the direction predicted by Van Creveld. The invasion of Ukraine has revealed a Kremlin directed by the so-called *siloviki,* "security men," and the former head of Wagner, Yevgeny Prigozhin, claimed that the invasion of Ukraine was not an outcome of NATO encroachment or resurgent Russian imperialism but, rather, an adventure promoted by the *siloviki* to enrich themselves.

8. See Gregory F. Treverton, Matt Wollman, Elizabeth Wilke, and Deborah Lai, *Moving Toward the Future of Policing* (Santa Monica, CA: RAND Corporation National Security Research Division, 2011).

9. It will not be a surprise to learn that the first deployments of special weapons units for police work occurred in colonial contexts such as Ireland (the Auxiliary Division) and Shanghai (the Reserve Unit) where policing was more concerned with pacification than public order. But a clearer line can be traced from contemporary SWAT teams to 1960s Los Angeles. In the wake of the Watts Riots, a special weapons unit was formed to engage in counterinsurgency warfare with US citizens. Since the 1960s, American policing has been meaningfully reshaped by heavily armed patrol officers who resort to violence too quickly and too often, and they are now supported by units that specialize in violence. Moreover, thanks to the defense sector's 1033 Program—the so-called Pentagon Pipeline—excess military equipment is transferred to the most bellicose branches of law enforcement.

10. See Vicky Conway's *Policing Twentieth Century Ireland* for discussion of the numerous scandals that rocked the Garda Síochána, some of which were enabled by the institution's self-

presentation as a local community police force. See also Luis Daniel Gascon and Aaron Roussell, *The Limits of Community Policing: Civilian Power and Police Accountability in Black and Brown Los Angeles* (New York: New York University Press, 2019).

11. H. Alker Tripp, "Police and Public: A New Test of Police Quality," *Police Journal* 1, no. 4 (1928): 529–539, passim.

CONCEPT NOTE: SOLUTIONISM

1. Of course, one could argue that solutionism has been evident since the dawn of the Enlightenment. After all, Jeremy Bentham's panoptic prison project was an architectural expression of solutionism underpinned by utilitarianism. Notably, Bentham's comments on "indirect means" of preventing crimes begin with the problem of monitoring ex-prisoners, addressing concerns such as mobility and privacy, before recommending every Englishman's arm be tattooed with an identification number, with legislation compelling the population to go about with a short sleeve on the tattooed arm. See Jeremy Bentham, *The Correspondence of Jeremy Bentham*, Vol. III, ed. Ian R. Christie (London: UCL Press, 2017).

2. Cedric G. Johnson, *After Black Lives Matter: Policing and Anti-Capitalist Struggle* (London and New York: Verso, 2023.).

3. Evgeny Morozov, *To Save Everything, Click Here: The Folly of Technological Solutionism* (New York: Public Affairs, 2013).

CHAPTER 4

1. See Mark Maguire and Reka Pétercsák, "Airports, from Vital Systems to Nervous Systems," in *Routledge Handbook of Anthropology and the City*, ed. Setha Low, 129–142 (London: Routledge, 2018).

2. European airport security also took shape in response to a specific incident. In May 1972, twenty-six people, mainly Puerto Ricans, were murdered in Tel Aviv Airport by a member of the Japanese Red Army working on behalf of a Palestine liberation group.

3. During the 1940s, for example, nationalists, fascists, communists, and anarchists described one another as radicalized lunatics. Exasperated, one French philosopher complained, "Ce terme de radicalization est vague."

4. See MI5, *Behavioral Science Unit Operational Briefing Note: Understanding Radicalization and Violent Extremism in the UK*. Report no. BSU 02/2008, 2008. See the leaked section at: http://image.guardian.co.uk/sys-files/Guardian/documents/2008/08/20/mi5.pdf. Few researchers have interviewed large numbers of committed terrorists firsthand. Those who have are in broad agreement with the MI5 report. See also Scott Atran, *Talking to the Enemy: Violent Extremism, Sacred Values, and What It Means to be Human* (London and New York: Penguin Books, 2011); also, Anne Speckhard and Molly D. Ellenberg, "ISIS in Their Own Words," *Journal of Strategic Security* 13, no. 1 (2020): 82–127.

5. Peter Neumann and Scott Kleinman, "How Rigorous Is Radicalization Research?" Democracy and Security 9, no. 4 (2013): 360–382.

6. William Shawcross, *Independent Review of Prevent* (London: Stationery Office, 2023), 11, 110.

7. See for examples Mark Maguire and David A. Westbrook, *Getting through Security: Counterterrorism, Bureaucracy, and a Sense of the Modern* (London and New York: Routledge, 2020).

8. For one among many examples of critical research on community policing, see Luis Daniel Gascon and Aaron Roussell, *The Limits of Community Policing: Civilian Power and*

Police Accountability in Black and Brown Los Angeles (New York: New York University Press, 2019).

CONCEPT NOTE: SECURITY-INDUSTRIAL COMPLEX

1. See Barry Buzan, *People, States and Fear: The National Security Problem in International Relations* (London: Wheatsheaf Books, 1983).

2. George F. Kennan, "Foreword," in *The Pathology of Power* by Norman Cousins, 9–17 (London and New York: W. W. Norton, 1988).

CHAPTER 5

1. The Group of Personalities was initially cochaired by Philippe Busquin, EU Commissioner for Research, and Erkki Liikanen, EU Commissioner for Enterprise and the Information Society. The group included chairpersons and CEOs of eight security companies (e.g., France's Thales and the UK's BAE Systems), four Members of the EU Parliament, four heads of research institutes, and a handful of former and serving high-level officials in key policy areas.

2. Group of Personalities (GoP), *Research for a Secure Europe: Report of the Group of Personalities in the Field of Security Research* (Luxembourg: Office for Official Publications of the European Communities, 2004), 7–11 passim.

3. See "INDECT" (2012). https://www.youtube.com/watch?v=9gVBFJg1AbA.

4. See European Commission (EC), "Answer to Anonymous on INDECT" (2012). Accessed January 24, 2022. https://www.youtube.com/watch?v=eJlNaScu6OQ.

5. Rory Stewart and Gerald Knaus, *Can Intervention Work?* (New York: W. W. Norton, 2011).

CONCLUSION

1. Maya Angelou, "Rehearsal for a Funeral," *The Black Scholar* 6, no. 9 (1975): 4.

2. See Angela Davis, "Freedom Struggle," *Democracy Now,* September 7, 2020. https://www.democracynow.org/2020/9/7/freedom_struggle_angela_davis_on_calls.

3. Graham Green, *The Quiet American* (London and New York: Penguin Books, 2004), 147.

4. Stephanie Carvin, "How Not to War," International Affairs 98, no. 5 (2022): 1713.

REFERENCES

Adey, Peter, Laure Brayer, Damien Masson, Patrick Murphy, Paul Simpson, and Nicolas Tixier. "Pour votre tranquillite: Ambiance, Atmosphere, and Surveillance." *Geoforum* 49 (2013): 299–309.

Allen, John. "Berlin's Potsdamer Platz and the Seductive Logic of Public Spaces." *Urban Studies* 43, no. 2 (2006): 441–455.

Altheide, David L. "Notes towards a Politics of Fear." *Journal for Crime, Conflict and the Media* 1, no. 1 (2003): 37–54.

Angelou, Maya. "Rehearsal for a Funeral." *The Black Scholar* 6, no. 9 (1975): 3–7.

Atran, Scott. *Talking to the Enemy: Violent Extremism, Sacred Values, and What It Means to Be Human*. London and New York: Penguin Books, 2011.

Bentham, Jeremy. *The Correspondence of Jeremy Bentham,* Vol. III. Edited by Ian R. Christie. London: UCL Press, 2017.

Brash, Julian. *Bloomberg's New York: Class and Governance in the Luxury City*. Athens: University of Georgia Press, 2011.

Brown, Wendy. *Walled States, Waning Sovereignty*. New York: Zone Books, 2010.

Butler, Octavia. *Parable of the Sower*. New York: Grand Central Publishing, (1998) 2019.

Buzan, Barry. *People, States and Fear: The National Security Problem in International Relations*. London: Wheatsheaf Books, 1983.

Carvin, Stephanie. "How Not to War." *International Affairs* 98, no. 5 (2022): 1695–1716.

Clarke, Katherine. "The Luxury Tower Built for New York's Elite Still Sits Half Empty." *Wall Street Journal,* July 13, 2023.

Conway, Vicky. *Policing Twentieth Century Ireland: A History of An Garda Síochána*. London and New York: Routledge, 2014.

Corsín Jiménez, Alberto, and Chloe Nahum-Claudel. "The Anthropology of Traps: Concrete Technologies and Theoretical Interfaces." *Journal of Material Culture* 24, no. 4 (2019): 383–400.

Davis, Angela. "Freedom Struggle." *Democracy Now,* September 7, 2020. https://www.democracynow.org/2020/9/7/freedom_struggle_angela_davis_on_calls.

Engels, Frederick. "Letter to Karl Marx, 25 May 1853." In *Karl Marx and Frederick Engels: Ireland and the Irish Question*, edited by Richard Dixon. Moscow: Progress Publishers, 1971.

European Commission (EC). "Answer to Anonymous on INDECT" (2012). Accessed January 24, 2022. https://www.youtube.com/watch?v=eJlNaScu6OQ.

Fassin, Didier. *Enforcing Order: An Ethnography of Urban Policing*. Cambridge: Polity Press, 2013.

Fawaz, Mona, Mona Harb, and Ahmad Gharbieh. "Living Beirut's Security Zones: An Investigation of the Modalities and Practice of Urban Security." *City & Society* 24, no. 2 (2012): 173–195.

Flynn, Rob, and Paul Bellaby. *Risk and the Public Acceptance of New Technologies*. London: Palgrave Macmillan, 2007.

Freund, David M. P. *Colored Property: State Policy and White Racial Politics in Suburban America*. Chicago: University Chicago Press, 2007.

Gamerman, Amy. "The New Gated Community: More Land, Fewer Neighbors." *Wall Street Journal*, August 24, 2017. https://www.wssj.com/articles/the-new-gated-community -more-land-fewer-neighbors-1503579674?tesla=y.

Gascon, Luis Daniel, and Aaron Roussell. *The Limits of Community Policing: Civilian Power and Police Accountability in Black and Brown Los Angeles*. New York: New York University Press, 2019.

Gay, Mara. "To Cut New York Housing Costs, Ease Suburb's Zoning Laws." *New York Times*, Opinion. February 23, 2023, A22.

Gilliard, Chris. "The Rise of 'Luxury Surveillance.'" *The Atlantic*, October 18, 2022. https://www.theatlantic.com/technology/ archive/2022/10/amazon.

Ginges, Jeremy, and Scott Atran. "Humiliation and the Inertia Effect: Implications for Understanding Violence and Compromise in Intractable Intergroup Conflicts." *Journal of Cognition and Culture* 8, no. 3/4 (2008): 281–294.

Gluck, Zoltan. "Security Urbanism and the Counterterror State of Kenya." *Anthropological Theory* 17, no. 3 (2017): 297–321.

Graham, Stephan, and Simon Marvin. *Splintering Urbanism: Networked Infrastructures, Technological Mobilities, and the Urban Condition*. London: Routledge, 2001.

Green, Graham. *The Quiet American*. London and New York: Penguin Books, 2004.

Group of Personalities (GoP). *Research for a Secure Europe: Report of the Group of Personalities in the Field of Security Research*. Luxembourg: Office for Official Publications of the European Communities, 2004.

Hobbes, Thomas. *Leviathan*. Oxford: Clarendon Press, (1651) 1909.

INDECT. "INDECT" (2012). Accessed January 24, 2022. https://www.youtube.com/watch?v=9gVBFJg1AbA.

Johnson, Cedric G. *After Black Lives Matter: Policing and Anti-Capitalist Struggle*. London and New York: Verso, 2023.

Jones, Terry. "The Police in America: A Black Viewpoint." *The Black Scholar* 9, no. 2 (1977): 22–39.

Kahlenberg, Richard. *Excluded: How Snob Zoning, Nimbyism, and Class Bias Build the Walls We Don't See*. New York: Public Affairs, 2023.

Kayden, Jeremy. *Privately Owned Public Space: The New York Experience*. New York: Wiley, 2000.

Kennan, George F. "Foreword." In *The Pathology of Power* by Norman Cousins, 9–17. London and New York: W. W. Norton, 1988.

Kimmelman, Michael. "Hudson Yards Is Manhattan's Biggest, Newest, Slickest Gated Community: Is This the Neighborhood New York Deserves?" *New York Times*, March 14, 2019.

Lang, Robert L., and K. A. Danielson. "Gated Communities in America." *Housing Policy Debate* 8, no. 4 (1997): 867–899.

Le Goix, Renaud, and Elena Vesselinow. "Inequality Shaping Processes and Gated Communities in the US Western Metropolitan Areas." *Urban Studies* 52 (2015): 619–638.

Levine, Yasha. *Surveillance Valley: The Secret Military History of the Internet*. New York and London: Public Affairs, 2018.

Lianos, Michalis. "Social Control after Foucault." *Surveillance & Society* 1, no. 3 (2003): 412–430.

Low, Setha. *Behind the Gates: Life, Security, and the Pursuit of Happiness in Fortress America*. New York: Routledge, 2003.

Low, Setha. "Towards a Theory of Urban Fragmentation: A Cross-Cultural Analysis of Fear, Privatization, and the State." *Cybergeo: Revue européenne de géographie,* Article 349, October 2, 2006.

Low, Setha. *Why Public Space Matters*. New York and London: Oxford University Press, 2023

Low, Setha, and Zoltan Gluck. "A Sociospatial Framework for the Anthropology of Security." *Anthropology Theory* 17, no. 3 (2017): 281–296.

Low, Setha, and Mark Maguire, eds. *Spaces of Security: Ethnographies of Security-scapes, Surveillance, and Control.* New York: New York University Press, 2019.

Maguire, Mark, and Pete Fussey. "Sensing Evil: Counterterrorism, Techno-science, and the Cultural Reproduction of Security." *Focaal: Journal of Global and Historical Anthropology* 75, no. 3(2016): 31–44.

Maguire, Mark, and Reka Pétercsák. "Airports, from Vital Systems to Nervous Systems." In *Routledge Handbook of Anthropology and the City*, edited by Setha Low, 129–142. London and New York: Routledge, 2018.

Maguire, Mark, and David A. Westbrook, *Getting through Security: Counterterrorism, Bureaucracy, and a Sense of the Modern.* London and New York: Routledge, 2020.

Marx, Karl. "On the Jewish Question" (1843). In *The Marx-Engels Reader,* edited by Robert Tucker, 26–46. New York: W. W. Norton & Co., 1978.

Masco, Joseph. *The Theater of Operations.* Durham, NC: Duke University Press, 2014.

Mattern, Sharon. "Instrumental City: The View from Hudson Yards, circa 2019." *Places*, April 2016.

MI5. *Behavioral Science Unit Operational Briefing Note: Understanding Radicalization and Violent Extremism in the UK.* Report no. BSU 02/2008, 2008. See the leaked section at: http://image.guardian.co.uk/sys-files/Guardian/documents/2008/08/20/mi5.pdf.

Mitchell, Don, and Lynn A. Staeheli. "Clean and Safe? Property Redevelopment, Public Space, and Homelessness in Downtown San Diego." In *The Politics of Public Space*, ed.

Setha Low and Neil Smith, 143–175. New York: Routledge, 2005.

Morozov, Evgeny. *To Save Everything, Click Here: The Folly of Technological Solutionism.* New York: Public Affairs, 2013.

Nemeth, Jeremy. "Lost Space: Security Zones and New York City's Shrinking Public Space." *International Journal of Urban and Regional Research* 34, no. 1 (2010): 20–34.

Neocleous, Mark. *Critique of Security.* Edinburgh: Edinburgh University Press.

Neumann, Peter, and Scott Kleinman. 2013. "How Rigorous Is Radicalization Research?" *Democracy and Security* 9, no. 4 (2008): 360–382.

Osman, Suleiman. "'We're Doing It Ourselves': The Unexpected Origins of New York City's Public-Private Parks during the 1970s Fiscal Crisis." *Journal of Planning History* 16, no. 30 (2017): 162–174.

Rand, Ayn. *Atlas Shrugged.* New York: Dutton, 1957.

Rand, Ayn. *For the New Intellectual.* New York: Signet, 1963.

Rigakos, George S. *Security/Capital: A General Theory of Pacification.* Edinburgh: Edinburgh University Press, 2016.

Rothstein, Richard. *The Color of Law: A Forgotten History of How Our Government Segregated America.* New York: W. W. Norton, 2017.

Rousseau, Jean-Jacques. *A Discourse on Inequality.* New York: The Philosophical Library, 2016.

Røyrvik, Emil. "The Sociality of Securitization: Symbolic Weapons of Mass Deception." *iNtergraph* 2, no. 2 (2010): 1–14.

Sanchez, Tom, and Robert L. Lang. "Security versus Status: The Two Worlds of Gated Communities." *Census Note 02:02.* Alexandria: Metropolitan Institute at Virginia Tech, 2002.

Sassen, Saskia. *The Global City: New York, London, Tokyo*. Princeton, NJ: Princeton University Press, 2001.

Seaton, Elizabeth. "The Commodification of Fear." *Topias* 5 (2018): 1–19.

Shawcross, William. *Independent Review of Prevent*. London: Stationery Office, 2023.

Simpson, Troy. "Open to the Public(s): A Critical Examination of Public Space in the Smart City." Dissertation proposal (updated), Environmental psychology. The Graduate Center, City University of New York, (2019) 2022.

Sloterdijk, Peter. *In the World Interior of Capital: Towards a Philosophical Theory of Globalization*. London and New York: Polity Press, 2013.

Smithsimon, Greg. "Dispersing the Crowd: Bonus Plazas and the Creation of Public Space." *Urban Affairs Review* 43, no. 3 (2008): 325–351.

Speckhard, Anne, and Molly D. Ellenberg. "ISIS in Their Own Words." *Journal of Strategic Security* 13, no. 1 (2020): 82–127.

Steel, M., and M. Symes. "The Privatization of Public Space? The American Experience of Business Improvement Districts and Their Relationship to Local Governance." *Local Government Studies* 31, no. 3 (2005): 321–334.

Stewart, Rory, and Gerald Knaus. *Can Intervention Work?* New York: W. W. Norton, 2011.

Tocqueville, Alexis de. *Journeys to Ireland and England*. Edited by J. P. Mayer. Translated by George Lawrence and J. P. Mayer. New Haven, CT: Yale University Press, 1958.

Treverton, Gregory F., Matt Wollman, Elizabeth Wilke, and Deborah Lai. *Moving toward the Future of Policing*. Santa Monica, CA: RAND Corporation National Security Research Division, 2011.

Tripp, H. Alker. "Police and Public: A New Test of Police Quality." *Police Journal* 1, no. 4 (1928): 529–539.

Uberoy, Urvashi, and Keith Collins. "New Yorkers Got Broken Promises. Developers Got 20 Million Sq. Ft." *New York Times*, July 21, 2023.

Van Creveld, Martin. *The Transformation of War.* London and New York: The Free Press, 1991.

Vitale, Alex S. *The End of Police.* New York and London: Verso, 2017.

Ward, Kevin. "Creating a Personality for Downtown: Business Improvement Districts in Milwaukee." *Urban Geography* 28, no. 8 (2007): 781–808.

Warner, Michael. *Publics and Counter-publics.* New York: Zone Books, 2002.

Yeats, William Butler. *The Winding Stair and Other Poems.* London: Scribner, (1933) 2011.

Zuboff, Shoshana. *The Age of Surveillance Capitalism: The Fight for a Human Future at the New Frontier of Power.* New York and London: Profile Books, 2019.

Printed in the USA
CPSIA information can be obtained
at www.ICGtesting.com
JSHW021128260124
55980JS00001B/1

9 781503 632967